Picture a determined red-haired woman in rubber pants with a little patch of lamb fuzz pinned to her chest. So stands Jessica Maxwell, resisting the powerful currents of the Deschutes River as it attempts to block her progress in casting to a hungry rainbow trout.

Fly fishing is a world of exasperating dilemmas and exhilarating triumphs, and Jessica Maxwell tangles her line in any number of them in this exuberant, witty account of learning to "fish first for the joy of it." Hopscotching from a series of Western rivers to outer Mongolia, Maxwell vividly chronicles the traditions and the idiosyncracies of the pastime and its curious subculture. Along the way, she explores the rich eddies of women in nature, the language of rivers, the importance of "learning to think like a fish," and the elusive state of grace she calls "quantum fishing." At times, fly fishing opens surprising emotional doors— leading to meditations on her relationship with her angler-father, as well as wry observations on being a girl in an almost all-boy fraternity.

In these pages, veteran anglers will see their sport through new eyes, and the many women who have newly embraced fly fishing will now have a voice, a guide, a fishing comrade of their own in Jessica Maxwell.

I DON'T KNOW WHY
I SWALLOWED THE FLY

MY FLY FISHING
ROOKIE SEASON

JESSICA MAXWELL

AN AVON BOOK

AVON BOOKS, INC.
1350 Avenue of the Americas
New York, New York 10019

The Sasquatch Books edition contains the following Library of Congress Cataloging in Publication Data:

Maxwell, Jessica, 1955-
   I don't know why I swallowed the fly / Jessica Maxwell.
      p.   cm.
1. Fly fishing—anecdotes. 2. Maxwell, Jessica, 1955-   I. Title.
SH456.M34   1997   96-3005
799.1'757—dc21

First Bard Printing: August 1998

For Mother and Bob

ACKNOWLEDGMENTS

Written in a little house in the big woods, this book thrived on daily electronic communion with its author's far-flung tribe, seasonal pow-wows with her siblings, and a standing dinner invitation from her parents, the best neighbors a girl-recluse ever had. A river of gratitude flows for the care of long-haul soul-sisters Lauri Doyle (27 years), Rande Lisle (23 years), and Bonnie Duncan (12 years); latter-day confidants Susan Ewing, Pat Barry, and Lee Rahr; and the Eugene Divine Arrangement Committee, Dottie Chase and June Jackson. For the deep-water guy-strength of fish brothers Guido Rahr, Rich Chapple, Rick Wendland, Terry Williams, Jim Youngren, Milt Fischer, Greg Tatman, Tim Spear, and Steve Smith; for the elegant tutoring of surrogate fishing fathers Len Dick and Roger Bachman; and the tireless passion of stellar wild fish reporter Clem Chapple: May your salmon return always and spawn often. For the awesome inspiration of the American ichthyologic illuminati: Lorian Hemingway, David James Duncan, Randy Wayne White, Tom McGuane, Lyla Foggia, Ted Leeson, Ted Strong, John Gierach, Larry Edfelt, Dave Hughes, Jennifer Olsson, John Holt, Ray Troll, and Brad Matsen: Fish Worship 'Til You Die, Y'all. For the blues imperative of fishing compadres Taj Mahal and Danny O'Keefe. For adZenture partners Russ and Blyth Carpenter and Yvon Chouinard, good luck charm Dave Moskowitz, best breakfast chef and genius fish poet David Campiche, soul-gardening guru Terry Hershey, miracles on the water with Fletcher Little, and the heart-and-mind super-glue of the University of Washington Advanced Literary Non-Fiction Class of '95—may the party never end. For research and supply-side support from the beloved SOI staff, Mike Treadway, Wayne Brown, Trenda LoVette, and Theresa Groff; Doug Ingoldsby and All One People; The Winston Rod Company; Cal Cole and Oregon Trout; John Sayre and Long Live the Kings; R.C. and The Pacific Salmon Foundation; Bill Bakke and the Native Fish Society; Nina Bell and Northwest Environmental Advocates; and the royal family of Northwest sense and sensibilities, Pam and Paul Schell. A tsunami of thanks to guardian angel agent Mary Alice Kier, editors Saint Gary Luke and Rachel "Perfect Faith" Klayman, Chad "the-coolest-publisher-in-the-business" Haight and the remarkable staff of Sasquatch Books, with an extra round of applause for Marlene Blessing and Holly Morris, who have the grace to cheer from opposing teams. Endless fish kisses to my sisters, Valerie Maxwell and Heather Meeker, who named this book in a fit of Christmas glee; to my nephew Jesse Maxwell "Tree Frog" Wilson, the best adventure partner ever; my nuclear niece, Amber Magdalena "Water Bug" Wilson; my brothers-in-law, Scott Wilson and John Beal, unflagging fountains of familial humor, dearest step-mother Zelma Maxwell, goddaughter Jessica Buskirk, forever sister-in-law Nancy Long, and Tillie, the sinking fishing corgi; and my spirit-sister Rande for coming through for me even in Class 3 rapids. The Golden Steelhead Award goes to my parents, Drs. Robert and Mary Meeker, who literally made everything possible.

CONTENTS

≈≈≈

One
River Deep, Mountain High **1**

Two
The Net **17**

Three
Dr. Dick's Change of Direction **27**

Four
The Blue Hour **47**

Five
"I Don't Know Why I Swallowed the Fly" **61**

Six
Bite the Wax Tadpole **83**

Seven
Our Father **113**

Eight
Quantum Fishing **127**

Nine
Girlfriends in the Fish Zone **149**

Ten
White Wings in the Morning **163**

Eleven
The Fish of 10,000 Casts **187**

Chapter One

RIVER DEEP, MOUNTAIN HIGH

A million gallons of water pressed hard against my thighs. Ancient rock cliffs soul-kissed the sky above me. Every move I made had distinct dinosaurean qualities. Every step I took seemed to take eons. I felt like Tina Turner trapped in a Paleozoic music video. What was I doing on the wrong side of Oregon standing in the middle of the Deschutes River with nothing to hold onto but the butt-end of a fly rod?

Trying to learn to fly fish, that's what. Which was why my fishing coach had parked me here in this flamboyant piece of fast water. Somehow I was supposed to complete an entomologically correct assessment of an invisible insect hatch, tie the appropriate caddis-whatever to the end of an invisible fly line, and make my linguini of a fly rod cast with impeccable accuracy to the waiting mouth of the invisible trout I had managed to spot in the Mount Vesuvius current blasting along in front of me. And I was expected to do all this without getting knocked on my neoprened derriere. But the truth was that nothing in my fishing life had prepared me for the relentlessness of rivers.

I grew up surf fishing in Southern California on the deckled edge of the American left coast, and became by default a person of oceanic rhythms. Waves build and crest and break with a one-two-three waltzing grace. The spaces between them let you breathe, little aquatic mezzanines where your mind can sit back, put its feet up, smoke a cigar.

Rivers offer anglers no such luxury. They hit the ground running, and run nonstop, twenty-four hours a day, year after panting year, and you are expected to keep up with them. This, I think, explains the inherent hyperactivity of fly fishing, the merciless casting, the endless exchange of one perfectly good fishing hole for another, the chronic wading, when sitting on the dock of the bay, so to speak, would do just fine. This was not the peaceful sport I grew up with. Fly fishing was some kind of Attention Deficit Disorder . . . with hooks!

I missed the briny serenity of my youth. In general, West Coast water doesn't do anything fast on a regular basis. Waves continue their usual impersonation of western civilization (build, rise, fall), tides shift gears imperceptibly within the

Pacific motor, and most of the time the water itself just sits there and does a slow, Jell-O hula. So, when you step into the surf and cast a baited hook out beyond the breakers, you can count on a long, easy tour of duty. You stand facing the horizon like the Queen of the Beach, eyes filled with the blue plane of the sea that spreads out before you like an anonymous, magnificent future. You stand and take stock approvingly of this your saline kingdom, enjoying a watery leg massage calibrated to match your resting heartbeat while the surf sucks lazily on your line—often for hours—until it all finally ends with the climactic burst of a big fish taking your sardine to China.

To a novice fly-fisher ocean person, river rhythms feel manic. You cannot, for instance, go down to your local hardware store and buy a river tide table. Rivers don't make predictable changes; they are immune to the moon. This, I think, is why they felt unknowable to me, a foreign kingdom ruled by a force so distracted there was clearly no chance to have a real relationship with them.

Given the tumult of the situation, I reckoned the explosion of a fish hitting my fly would just seem like part of the scenery. I knew I'd miss it. Of course, that attitude might have had something to do with the fact that the only fish I'd ever hooked and landed in a river so far was a Mongolian lenok about the size of your average banana. As I recall, it wiggled at precisely the same velocity as both the riffle from whence it came and the alder leaves shimmying above it, obfuscating the entire experience, which was already blurred by the weirdness of its having occurred on the steppes of Outer

Mongolia, of all places.

It was there, in the shallows of Mongolia's Sharlon River, on the green, leafy fringe of the Siberian border, that my heart first thrilled to the high art of fly fishing. I was, after all, witnessing an artist: Guido Reinhardt Rahr III of Portland, Oregon, one of the most gifted young anglers in the Pacific Northwest.

Though we'd never met, Guido (pronounced "Ghee-dough," not "Gwee-dough") and I had both signed up for something called The First Western Fishing Expedition to Outer Mongolia. Under the auspices of a Seattle outfitter, fourteen of us fishing fanatics were going after the biggest "salmon" on earth—the species *Hucho hucho taimen,* which are actually giant trout that can weigh up to two hundred pounds.

At that point I had been an impassioned salmon fisher-woman in my own right for years, favoring an old British Columbia version of the sport called tyee fishing. It's done out of a rowboat and instead of bait uses classic Northwest tackle, such as wooden Lucky Louie plugs and metal "spoons." But, like the saltwater live-sardine bait fishing my father had taught me, when you're tyee fishing you just toss your lure into the water and wait. It was a far cry from the frenetic cast-and-step activity of fly fishing.

I was familiar with fly fishing back then. I'd had a few lessons and I liked fooling around with feathers and hooks, if only to make scary earrings. But the triumph of masterful an-gling was unknown to me until I saw Guido draw his delicate scrimshaw on the ivory underbelly of the arcing Mongolian sky. He stood there in the shallows of that exotic water, broad-shouldered, narrow-hipped, square-jawed, and tan. The bright Mongolian sun only amplified the male grace of his form. When he moved, gold flashed both from his cropped yellow hair and the metal rim of his glasses. But when he talked he sounded as though he were on TV.

"We're standing here on the far edge of farthest Outer Mongolia," he announced suddenly, punching out every syllable, "fishing for the BIGGEST salmonids on earth."

There wasn't a hint of farce in his voice, not a trace of irony, and no sign of self-consciousness anywhere. The young man was serious, and, as it turned out, he *was* on TV. He was talking into a video camera whose operator remained hidden behind a tree until I stepped a little closer and saw him.

"We're using giant Marabou Muddlers with spun deer-hair heads," Guido continued. Little coronas of spit now followed each word. "Because these fish are CARNIVORES, known to feed on mice and muskrats . . . even small dogs!"

With that he turned and, still on camera, resumed his exuberant, powerful casting, laying down one perfectly straight line after another with the precision of a French pastry chef. Never had a Mongolian river received such lavish decoration. Never had a *National Geographic* scouting video inspired such a bravura performance. And never had I beheld such an act of aerial finesse.

Until that moment, fly fishing remained a distant distraction, a rarefied adjunct to the broader sport I'd loved all my life. But when I saw the way Guido's line moved, its impossible lengths suspended for whole moments above the surface

of the river before its business-end dropped its fly exactly
where he wanted it—well, I knew then that I knew nothing
of the soul of this sport I had taken so lightly. Like the African
tribe that has no word for God other than the blowy sound
of "whew," I said as much myself, sat down on the ancient
Mongolian earth, and watched for all I was worth.

Observing Guido cast gave me an uncomfortable sense of
comfort. For a moment I couldn't figure out why. Then it hit
me: my father. As a child I had spent hours watching my father cast. Not the fore-and-aft continuum of fly casting, the
single long-bomb forward action of big saltwater reels. But
my father's rod cut the air the same way, and his line always
shot out to kingdom come, just like Guido's. Even their pos-
tures were similar: the strongly planted feet, the athlete's hips,
the rocking right shoulder, the sure brown hands, the eyes
that never left the far end of the rod. I knew that posture as
well as I knew anything about my father. It must have imprinted itself deeply on my mind during the early years—
from piers, from beaches, from the uneven granite plates of
coastal outcroppings. It was as if all the love and all the pain
between fathers and daughters were locked into that form—
its sweet familiarity, and its distance. When Daddy fished he
was happy, but he was also always Over There. It was, I think,
his therapy in those pre-therapist days. My mother is a cul-
tured woman, nourished wholly by art, literature, and a beautiful home. But the only thing that gave my father peace of
mind was the thing that cut him off from me: the solitude of
fishing.

In any weather, any season, if he were staring at the tip of a fishing rod, my father was happy. The heavens could un-leash pit-bull monsoons that sent saner campers to their tents, and my father would still be fishing. The fiercest wind could send those tents cartwheeling down the beach, and my father would still be fishing. The truth is, while we had fished to-gether throughout my childhood, by the time I took up the rod again as an adult, my father was too infirm to go fishing with me, racked as he was by emphysema. On fishing trips I took along instead my most powerful memory of him: his lone form standing on the end of an old rock jetty, casting over and over into the wild blue California yonder.

I was raised in a beach town when they were still beach towns and not the suburbs of Los Angeles. It was the late fifties, and the air did not yet sit on the ocean like yellow grease. On Sundays our father often walked my sister and me down the long Manhattan Beach pier and claimed a spot in the clear blue air around the strange roundhouse snack bar–bait shop at the pier's western end, from which we caught mackerel or bar-racuda or banjo shark with live sardines that cost the same as a Big Hunk, except that you had to catch them yourself, which my sister and I thought was the best fishing of all. We picked out the fish we wanted, and, being the eldest, I chased it around with a dip net until my eyes lost it when it passed other sardines that looked suspiciously like itself. Then my sister said, "No, *that* one," and got me back on track until, finally, we proudly offered our catch to our father in a white Chinese food container filled with salt water. And that was always the end of our intimacy with it, because he never expected us to poke a hook through the nose of a pet sardine.

Our father was very clear on that. Had we been sons instead of daughters, his chivalry might have transmuted into a gory education. But it was still the fifties, and we were girls, and I'm sure he reckoned that our squeals would have disturbed the other fishermen who, like himself, were there to stare with complete concentration at the tips of their rods while the ashes of their cigarettes grew longer and longer until they crash-landed in purified piles on the dried sardine blood and ossified fish guts that laminated the cement surface of the old Manhattan Beach pier. In the summer we abandoned pier fishing and drove south to the hillside town of Palos Verdes where we hiked down a certain cliff, which was the color of Dijon mustard, not green. The cliff path ended at Bluff Cove, an off-center half-moon of water whose right curve rose onto a pocked plateau that shot straight into the ocean.

When the tide was out, the plateau became a landscape of child-sized saltwater lakes. That was when our father lit a cigarette, stationed himself on the sight of that granite gun barrel, and held his particular piece of the Pacific ransom. He wanted its rockfish, its coppers and cow cod, and he would stand out there all day firing his baited bullets into the boiling target while the surf fired back at him, encircling his form again and again with frothy shrapnel.

While our father fished, my sister and I played in the tide-pools, a sport we never tired of. Our father had taught us the secret: move too fast and you miss things; pay attention and everything comes to life. It remains to this day my own First Law of Fishing . . . of everything.

~~~~

It was riveting work, peering like God into whole worlds you
did not create, watching for diminutive sculpin and baby oc-
topus. But every so often I looked up to check on our father
standing out there on his private peninsula while the white
hands of the surf tried again and again to drag him under.
They always failed and fell back in despair, leaving him with
salty haloes around his head, as if he were an angel for having
daughters, not sons, and not regretting it.

It was our good fortune that he just went ahead and treated
us like sons, teaching us to do the things he himself had learned
to love as a kid growing up in New Zealand—camping, hunting, and most especially, fishing. Like Guido's angling, our father's was a sight to behold. When he fished, all his nervous
energy drained out his hands, and, traveling at the speed of
thought, ran up his fishing rod, transferred to the geometry of
his line, and was simply thrown away. All of his pain—his own
father's early death, the orphanage, the war, the divorce—all of
it vanished and left him stilled, freed even, for whole hours at
a time. Witnessing my father finally at home in his own body
is, I think, what made me fall in love with fishing at such a
young age. It is, I know, what brought me back to it as an adult.

For vacations we took long driving trips, heading north
always, camping and fishing as we went. Maybe we made it to
the redwoods. Maybe the Oregon coast. Twice we got all the
way to Vancouver Island, and it was on those trips that I first
was charmed by the Pacific Northwest's malachite beauty.
Later I chose the region as my home, settling on one of the

little green islands in Puget Sound I had seen and loved from the ferry so many years before.

On that island the world outside my door is utterly different from the tawny open beaches of my childhood. It is self-contained and dense and very difficult to know. Its remnant forests are still threaded with silver stitches of water; indeed, water rules this boreal universe—lakes, fjords, rivers, the inland sea that surrounds my own island like a protective arm. And, of course, the rain.

When I left California in the seventies to go to school in Oregon, I fell madly in love with the rain. When I left California again in the eighties to move permanently to the Northwest, I was like a person dying of thirst and reaching for water. To this day my fixation on water borders on dementia. Some people carry a Saint Christopher's medal or a dolphin pendant as a talisman. I carry water. Always. Full liters in my car, a little bottle in my purse, even a tiny silver flask in evening bags that draws snorts of disbelief and disappointment when I say, "It's only water."

I never touch any of it. It's not for drinking. It's for having. Keeping. Because nothing sends me into a panic faster than running out of water. I can't explain it, really. It would be easy to say it has something to do with security or health, as the world continues to poison its supply of drinking water, but I suspect something a lot closer to home. I am convinced that water is the key to understanding a landscape on which the sky weeps nine months of the year.

Here in the Northwest, water feels charged with the possibilities of birth fluid. In the half-light of winter, dark and wet

as a womb, fish emerge from our rivers and streams as if just
born. They look, and feel to the touch, more like congealed
water than the animals they are. Their link to the land is in-
escapable. They evolved with it, surviving ice age after ice age,
riding the geographic changes as they came, colonizing and re-
colonizing streams and rivers as they charted and recharted
their courses. Fish grew up with the place, and ever since I myself arrived, I have not been able to divine a better way of understanding this piece of watery earth than to fish it.

Like the finest umbilicus, casting your line into water
joins you to it. The currents speak to your bones in iced
tongues. The loam perfume of conifer rot and mud attunes
your nose to the local biology. You taste its chemistry, wash
your ears in its sweet white noise, let it take you back to a
time before words and teach you things language never could.

My father was a bait fisherman, a man of salt and surf.
The ocean still has a powerful hold on me, and always will.
But when I saw the cursive grace of Guido Rahr's fly line
writing prayers I couldn't read to the river gods of Outer
Mongolia, I knew my name was written there too. Fly fishing was going to be my version of my father's sport, my nod
to my Scottish ancestors and to myself, and to the fish-crazed
part of America I had claimed as my own. That night, when
the campfire smoke sent its own cryptic messages heavenward, I asked Guido if he would teach me how to fly fish
once we were back in the Northwest. Like the brother I
never had, he said yes.

Of course I had no idea how much effort went into serious fly fishing. And knowledge. Raw skill, and instinct, balance,

strength and undiluted concentration. Not to mention equipment: waders, wading boots, fly vests, shortie rain jackets,
several sizes of rods, reels with several sizes of line, all kinds
of tools, Polaroid glasses, a hundred kinds of flies, and a thousand kinds of feathers and fur if you dare to tie your own. No
wonder Daddy stuck to one-rod/one-reel saltwater fishing
with sardines. Learning how to fly fish was going to take
years!

What a joke. I'd taken up this crazy sport specifically to
get to know the grand, green Pacific Northwest, and there I
was on the inland side of the mountains floundering around
in a skinny spit of water in country that looked like the reason the Okies left Oklahoma. Fortunately I'm not one for de-
pressions, great or small, so I tried to find something good
about the place. Well, I thought, it's . . . not raining. Now *that*
was depressing. It's dry here, my mind warned. Real dry. I
reached for my water bottle.

Then I remembered that I was standing in water. Well,
that's a plus, I thought: you've always got enough water when
you're standing in a river. This piece of radical intelligence
cheered me considerably—until Guido showed up again and
ordered me out of the water.

"Time for Master's Eddy," he said, and made me hike
downstream with him another quarter mile, a real trick if
you're wearing a pair of clunkoid too-big sopping-wet wading boots. But I clomped along behind him like a trained
brontosaurus until he stopped short above a slowly undulat-
ing elbow of the river.

"There it is," Guido announced. "Master's Eddy."

From above, the place looked like a giant hurricane.

"It's one of the Deschutes' classic fishing holes," Guido advised me. "See all those little pink dots? Those are rising trout mouths. Master's Eddy is like a giant rotating insect buffet. The bugs get trapped in the currents there and just go around and around, and the fish just hang out and stuff themselves. So," he said with a courtly sweep of his hand, "start casting."

Good idea, I thought. But first I have to get down there. The bank above Master's Eddy is at almost a ninety-degree angle to the river and it's made largely of loose rock. So, while Guido stomped off to go fish somewhere by himself, I slowly worked my way downhill, feeling like Lucy trying to sneak up on Ricky's fishing party. An avalanche of stones telegraphed my progress to every fish within a two-mile radius. Soon I started skidding and ended up going the rest of the way sitting down. Then I virtually belly-flopped smack into the eye of the hurricane, scattering trout in all directions.

That done, I stopped to take a look around. I must say, the place had a style all its own. Unlike the bright turquoise plate of the Pacific, the basalt cradle that holds the Deschutes River looked spent, a beleaguered husk of a landscape that couldn't help but show its age: four million years and counting. Rushing hard out of the middle Cascade Mountains, the river drains the entire escarpment of central Eastern Oregon, but its mute palette of ochers and taupes is relieved only by silver bolls of sage and darker fans of juniper. Oaks hold forth stoically in the desiccated lowlands, but alders quake at the water's edge like refugees dying for a drink. Only the most

sophisticated of designers would find inspiration in the Deschutes' monochromatic, mineralized dust. In the dry light of
an autumn afternoon, standing in water again seemed like a
very good place to be, especially in the shadow of the volcanic
upheaval that cut the region off from water-bearing Pacific
storms in the first place. Though it's hardly the powerful presence of the Pacific, the mere existence of that youthful blue
line of river in that arid terrain seemed miraculous.

Encouraged, I tried to cast. But Master's Eddy is deep. I
couldn't wade out very far, and without much room for back-
casting, casting itself seemed impossible. I raised my rod and
carefully lowered it behind me, but its tip collided with the
bank. Guido had warned me that Master's Eddy was a tough
place to fish, but he blamed it on the currents, "which are always changing and you never know when or how," he had
said. The problem was that the river pushes against the rock
wall there and sends the water into ever-shifting spirals. And
that makes it difficult to get a good drift, according to Guido,
"because the water tends to push away from you without
warning and make your fly drag—a sure sign to a trout that
what appears to be a bug is really something weird."

All in all, it takes a master to master Master's Eddy, and
despite my supra-neophyte status, for some reason Guido
thought the practice would do me good. Probably because
that's where he himself had learned to fly fish decades before.

While the rest of the Deschutes continued its mad dash
north, I tried to figure out where I could position myself in
that watery sidewinder of a fishing hole so that I could cast
without floating away like a giant mayfly. My borrowed men's

boots swam around on the rocks and my feet swam around in my boots—sort of a swim/swim situation. More than once I almost went swimming myself, but Master's Eddy moves slowly, so you tend to fall in quietly and thus avoid disturbing the dozens of kissy pink trout mouths that do indeed stipple this merry smorbugasbord.

Having waded as deeply as I dared, I procured a precarious balance and cast. Sort of. I really still didn't know how to do it. So I tried to imitate my mental image of Guido's beautiful cast: I carefully lifted my line off the water, pulled my rod back to ten o'clock . . . and—zing!—became profoundly hung up in the brush behind me.

I slopped over to the bank and scuttled uphill, clinging to the falling-apart terrain like a neoprene leech. When I finally found my fly, I marveled at the shish kebob of leaf and branch I had made with one flick of a novice's wrist. Then I scrambled back down, slid into the water, and popped up like a breath mint, scattering the fish again.

Giving the ancient basalt a forty-mile stare, I waited until the greedy little trout mouths reappeared. Then I decided to try to execute a roll cast, which I didn't know how to do either. Again mimicking Guido, I drew my rod up until it pointed directly overhead, then slammed it down like a sledgehammer and ended up hooking my chin.

"Yeow!"

I slipped again. Holding my rod high in some bizarre half-reflex from my early salmon-fishing training, I began a slow, floating orbit around Master's Eddy like a narcissistic Statue of Liberty hooked only on herself.

Now, of course, is when Guido decided to come check on me. Somehow missing the compromised position of my mandible, he explained that the real action was to be found at Lunker Haven, the stretch of boulder water just around the bend. "I'll meet you there in about fifteen minutes," he said, "now that you've mastered Master's Eddy."

What I'd actually mastered is Fly Fishing Safety Rule #1: "Remove all hooks from soft tissue under water, where near–freezing temperatures anesthetize exposed nerve endings and you can't hear your fellow anglers' hyena laughter." Which at the moment was ricocheting off the Deschutes' old canyon walls like the ghostly voices of fly fishermen past, begging me to take up stamp collecting.

Chapter Two

THE NET

"There's a big fish in front of that rock."

Guido's announcement cut through Lunker Haven's noisy atmosphere like a temple bell. Veteran fly fishermen are forever whispering watery incantations like that, and, resonant as they are with promise and portent, novices generally find them highly irritating. Why a *big* fish? Why *that* rock? How the hell do *you* know, anyway?

But given my recent and miserable baptism in Master's Eddy, the certainty in Guido's words was a benediction, or perhaps more accurately, a life preserver—something solid to hold onto in fly fishing's world of increasingly slippery unknowables. Something, ultimately, that floats.

The rock supposedly hiding Guido's Big Fish was one of

many that knob that impressive stretch of white water. While the Deschutes circles quietly in Master's Eddy just upstream, it takes off at a sloppy gallop across Lunker Haven's tubercled countenance. Big boulder water, it's called, the thousand-year-old fallout from a gigantic geologic barf-a-thon that charged down Hidden Canyon, scattering basalt boulders as it went. The result is a tract of pocket water that makes most anglers feel like reaching into their own pocket to bet money on the presence of fish there.

"When the fish in Master's Eddy get bigger than sixteen or seventeen inches they move into Lunker Haven," Guido's voice intoned.

Amen.

"The boulders break the current and the fish like to sit in the soft pockets in front of them and behind them to conserve energy."

Say amen.

"We'll fish for them with a little orange bucktail caddis, and we'll fish with vigor and creativity."

Say amen, somebody!

Somebody did, because the next second Guido Reinhardt Rahr III stepped into the river, well-worn 6-weight Winston rod in hand, and cast what looked like a little piece of a Las Vegas showgirl headdress upstream. The festive fly landed dead-center in front of The Rock, and since we were standing behind it, I didn't see if The Fish hit the fly midair or at the precise moment of touchdown, but the water there exploded with wild force. Guido's old Winston did an instant 180, whipping from south to due north, a prayer flag in a typhoon. There was a definite change in the weather.

And in my angling education curriculum.

Because Guido, without asking or warning, handed off the aching rod to me.

"Play it," he commanded, meaning the fish.

There was hardly time to. The reel sang a screechy chant in a language that sounded like Tibetan. The fish headed for the Himalayas. Or, at least, Seattle. All I could do was hold on tight and keep my fingers out of the way of the reel handle, which had become a vicious little propeller determined to render the rod airborne and jet it downstream after the fish.

The fish continued its torpedo run toward the Columbia. We did our best to keep up with it, a couple of neurologically challenged mountain goats leaping unsteadily from boulder to boulder. Chasing a fish down a rocky river is one of angling's more indelicate acts of attrition. It is especially demanding if one has hooked a fish in high season on a popular river. I once witnessed a very nervous Japanese gentleman on a river in Southeast Alaska chase a forty-pound salmon past two dozen fellow anglers, each of whom received a polite bow and a heartfelt "excuse me" as he lifted his straining rod over every envious head.

Meanwhile, even on this deserted piece of river, Guido and I had a desperate time staying ahead of our own vanishing line. It was no use.

"Jeez," I said finally. "What *is* this?"

"It might be a steelhead," Guido panted. "I've never seen a trout do that."

What it had done—or was about to do—was spool me.

That is, take all of the line on the reel and leave me with an empty bobbin, a fast-forward pulse, and a broken heart. I had played enough salmon to know there was nothing I could do—this fish was on a mission. I asked anyway.

"What can I do?" I whined.

"Nothing," Guido replied. "Grab the reel."

"No!" I wailed. "No, please no!"

Grabbing the reel would stop the line and break it at its weakest part—the fine filament attached to the fly, called the tippet. But this was my first serious river fish. Rather, my first moment on-line with a serious river fish, and the sense of connection was brutal. I was thrilled. But, as always, I was also sickeningly aware that the fish was not. And that knowledge is the cloud in the silver lining that is my every fishing trip.

This was, I knew, one connection my fish surely wished it hadn't made—one, more to the point, it certainly didn't understand. Only Gary Larson could picture a fish leering up at a juicy-looking caddis fly, saying to itself: "Now, let's see . . . if I bite that thing, it'll either taste great or it will try to drag me out of the water by my lips. Well, that's the chance you take. I'm goin' for it."

Once it decided to strike, short of lousy angling technique the only chance this fish had was the one it was taking by racing downstream—and that's what a lot of non-anglers have against fishing.

"You tricked the poor fish," they say.

They, on the other hand, are almost never vegetarians and can easily be made to confess their delight in ordering, say, a slab of persimmony Copper River salmon in a huckleberry beurre blanc sauce at any of the Northwest's better dining establishments. Thus does Fish become Art, making a kind of conceptual leap in modern minds that manages to miss Food altogether. Mainly, I think, because somebody else did the dirty work, both the physical effort of ichthyological hunting-and-gathering and, finally, of lethal bonking.

"As long as someone else kills it, I'll eat it," nonvegetarians say. And that, in a crabshell, is what's wrong with western culture: the blind and blinding intellectual separation from the natural life-death-life systems that support it.

As fishing essayist Ted Leeson says in his elegant book *The Habit of Rivers:* everything lives at the expense of something else. Or as John Steinbeck concludes in *The Sea of Cortez:* everything eats everything.

"Not I," says the vegetarian. "I never eat anything that has a face." Yet two pounds of living, faceless carrots must die for every precious cup of carrot juice. And God knows how many salmon expired because of the lowered water level of the river that irrigated the farm that grew the carrots.

Is the life of a carrot truly worth less than the life of a fish? I'd hate to have to argue the point to a carrot. I even avoided it during my own ten-year stint as a vegetarian . . . until two facts became abundantly clear: (1) this Celtic body of mine is *not* a natural vegetarian, as demonstrated by a growing plethora of food allergies and fatigue due to liver dysfunction due to animal-protein deficiency; and (2) if I am a natural meateater, then I would be an honorable one, willing, at least, to fish for my supper. Guido makes sense when he says, "Let's take some responsibility for our protein." So when I'm asked what I eat, I say the same thing Alaska Iditarod super-musher Susan Butcher said when I asked her that question: "I eat a basic vegetarian diet—and moose." Or, in my case, fish.

The vegetarian-nonvegetarian question really pivots not on dietary concerns, but on the slender edge of our darkest fear: death. Death is big. Taking the life of anything is a very big deal indeed. The first time I caught a salmon I asked my fishing guide to let me kill it myself, because I knew I *had* to. So I raised his battered, bloodstained fish club and smacked the seventeen-pound chinook right on its beautiful silver-and-blue head. My aim was true. My fish died with a heart-stopping quiver. And I burst into tears. All the intended goodness that had been my life until then—my endless attempts to be kind, help others, save the world from suffocation-by-plastic wrap, and not yell at people who tell you you have to dial a different number after you were just on hold for ten minutes—all of it suddenly narrowed to that one point of violence. And the resulting moral dissonance threw my mind into a kind of spiritual anaphylactic shock. I sobbed inconsolably for the next twenty minutes.

When finally I composed myself, we headed out again. I caught a second salmon, a bigger one. This time I took a breath, said a silent prayer of gratitude, and struck the fish's bonny bony skull like a warrior. The transformation I underwent between the two killings was, I think, born of having crossed over from the Valley of the Urban Wimps into the Kingdom of Dzwonka, the Wild Woman of the Northwest coastal tribes whose whistling song you hear any time the wind passes through the trees. It is a far more honest place from which a nonvegetarian might hail.

Bushmen of the Kalahari probably would agree, and, until the recent African drought drove them into the cities, they were some of the most "natural"—and gentle—people left on earth. Remember when the Bushman dropped that antelope with a poison dart in *The Gods Must Be Crazy?* He didn't yell the Kalahari equivalent of "Oh, baby, I got me a big one . . . . Would ya look at that rack . . . . Whoooo-eeee!" Nor did he bemoan his angst, sniffling "Oh, now look what I've done! Oh, I'm *so sorry.* Oh no, oh, gee . . . ."

No, the quiet little man simply squatted on the old African earth beside the fallen animal, placed his hand on its horn, and talked to it for half an hour, explaining that his people needed meat and he was very grateful to it for providing it. He didn't enjoy killing for killing's sake, and he didn't nail the antelope's head to his hut wall, but he didn't shy away from the act of taking a life for life's sake, either. He understood death as an inevitable part of living.

All of which puts the practice of catch-and-release fishing in a dubious light and explains why more than one non-angler refers to it as "torture-and-release." But studies have proven that a properly released fish (i.e., kept *in* the water while handled, so its lactic acid readings don't rise to permanent and lethal levels) has more than a ninety percent chance of survival, whereas a properly bonked dinner-table fish has no chance of survival at all.

Furthermore, every angler I know purposely takes a fish's

life sometimes, if the run is strong enough to sustain the loss, or if it's a hatchery fish, as signified by a clipped fin or lip.

Of course, in order to decide whether to release or not release, one must first have a fish, and by all accounts, at that moment our steelhead-cum-macro-trout was already halfway to the Columbia. The reel's inner beauty was showing. My line was long gone. There was nothing left to do but grab the reel. So I did.

The resulting collapse of connection felt like what the Apollo 13 astronauts must have felt when they lost contact with Mission Control. Broken. Gone. The Big Nothing. I had every right to feel cheated, lonely and blue, and I thought I would . . . but instead I felt ecstatic. Because I had *felt* it. The fish. A fish. A real live big-league river fish. Never mind that I had nothing to do with hooking the thing, that, technically, it wasn't my fish at all, it was Guido's. It was my connection. Because I had felt it.

And connected I had been. When the fish changed directions, I felt it. When it slowed or sped up, I felt that too. It's such a raw thing, this shared existence with a piece of bucking biomass. A wild animal has a mind of its own. It will not consult you on its decisions, and even the benefit of a hook and line does not give you control. All you can do is react while the fish does what it can to survive.

The angler holds the life-and-death struggle in her hands. This is serious business. But this is not, really, what you think about when you've got a fish on the line. What you think about is that you have a fish on the line. Actually, not a whole lot of thinking goes on at all. When you've got a fish on the line you just feel it, like music, then move, like dance.

Fishing is a predator's cotillion. The steps are formalized, predictable. Unless it is spawned-out or very sick, a fish on a line is bound to resist. Unless she is asleep at the reel, an angler is bound to resist that resistance. The fish runs, the fisherman lets it but holds on tight. The fish runs far, the fisherman tries to turn its head. The fish turns and runs toward the boat, the fisherman reels in like a crazy person. Line tension is kept taut at all times, but not too taut. The rod tip is kept high, always.

These are the technicalities. The jetés and pirouettes. But the music of the dance lies in the subtle signals between the steps: the fish's delivery of them, the fisherman's read of and response to them, which, if she's good, must be near telepathic. *That's* what takes a death-grip on your concentration. That's why your mind empties of all trivia, which, when playing a fish, includes just about everything else you could possibly think of. That is what anglers live for. That's what my father knew, my salmon days had taught me that much.

A fish on the line so distills one's attention that time does a swift crash-and-burn. During those few on-line moments the fish's electric bio-engine runs everything, all a fisherman can do is try to stay in the game. If fly fishing is a meditation, then playing a fish is satori. You are aware only of awareness—the predator's genius. That's fishing.

To say that catching a fish is "exciting" renders the event intellectually anemic. There's a lot more racing blood to it than that. "Fascination has a gravity all its own," insists the Scottish golf guru Shivas Irons in Michael Murphy's *Golf in the Kingdom.* "It can draw upon the subtle forces, draw them round us lik' a cloak, and create new worlds."

Irons might as well have been talking about fly fishing. Having a fish on the line is like finding yourself in the hands of an energetic lover. The connection is in full swing, the heat is on, you are bound to that universe of two. What are you going to do? Slide out of bed and go get a beer? I don't think so. Unless something shorts out somewhere, you ride it through to the end. You cannot conceive of doing anything else at that moment other than what you're doing. It's the same with a fish on the line: the event is that fascinating, that overpowering. Like the very first time I connected to cyberspace and went online, the electricity of my first river fish contact was imprinted on my nerve sheaths forever. Once Guido handed me his shrieking Winston, bent in two as if in ecstatic prayer, there was no doubt about it, the fish in the net was I.

Chapter Three

DR. DICK'S CHANGE
OF DIRECTION

By morning the canyon was glazed with lilac light. The air was a western syrup, thick with the silver alkaloids of sage, the gin perfume of juniper. The old basalt hills rose softly to the east and west like a sleeping woman's hips, and along the river the alders seemed to have gone golden overnight. October on the Deschutes.

Desert landscapes have always scared me. They feel, despite their beauty and breadth, claustrophobic. Such is the curse of my seaside childhood: security resides in land's end, not land. If the earth does not drop off into a blue bowl, then I feel trapped, landlocked, and without breath, which is what the Hawaiian epithet for white person—*haole*—actually means.

The ocean makes its own atmosphere. Anyone who has ever driven west from downtown Los Angeles knows this. Just about the time you pass the exit for the Santa Monica Freeway, the air changes. It cools and fills with minerals, the vaporized salts of the Pacific. At that point ocean people realize they've been holding their breath; at that point we can breathe again.

To us the popular dream of moving to Montana is a nightmare without doors. Give me land lotsa land—only if it has a surefire escape route, a way to sail away; otherwise to hell with starry skies above. Standing even in the rarefied environment of Central Oregon, I was sure that a little riverish trickle couldn't possibly replace the deep relief an ocean offers, and I was about to tell as much to Dr. Dick, but he had just grabbed my fishing hand and rammed it into the purple air in front of my face.

"*Punch* it," he said. "It's a *punch*. That business about it all being in the wrist is a buncha B.S. Punch! Punch! Punch, dammit!"

Dr. H. Lenox H. Dick: Philadelphia native, Portland resident, retired physician, Quaker, reigning Old Man of the Deschutes River, and the most renowned curmudgeon on either side of the Cascades. He also happens to be both the author of the angling classic *The Art and Science of Fly Fishing,* and related by marriage to Guido Rahr through Guido's mother (she is Mrs. Dick's first cousin). Thus did my fishing coach summon the courage to ask the good doctor to indulge me in a rare private lesson. Much to Guido's surprise, he agreed. I was warned, however, to steel myself for cantankerous behavior.

Tall, exceptionally lean, white-haired and pink-cheeked, Dr. Dick has blue eyes that gleam with bad attitude. He is, for instance, so maniacally antismoking that everyone on the river has to hide their cigars from him or he'll throw them into the fireplace when nobody's looking. If it weren't for his directional dyslexia, which forever sends him stomping off in the wrong direction, and his hair, which looks as though he cuts it himself without a mirror, Len, as his friends call him, wouldn't have any endearing qualities.

Clearly, a lifetime of fishing the Deschutes—and his haircut—have kept him young, if not cordial. At eighty, Len Dick looks sixty and regularly startles women on the Deschutes by walking around with his fly unzipped. Dr. Dick is not, however, "trolling," as one newcomer meanly suggested. He is simply pragmatic, and wears khaki pants *over* his waders to protect them from branches and thorns, seeing no reason to bother zipping a zipper when one has an impenetrable layer of neoprene underneath. If one is not privy to this information, however, one might remain justifiably wary of the unzipped virility of an eighty-year-old who still rows his own boat across Class 2 rapids several times a day to get to and from his fishing retreat.

On the river, Dr. Dick's place is known as the old Fitzpatrick homestead, now a raw-boned, three-room, ramshackle wooden . . . well, shack, on thirty wide-open acres. Your mother would never stay there. But those who do, fall in love with its drastic cow-skull beauty—the little wood-stove, the worn-out floorboards, the dust. Ralph Lauren would kill for that kind of authenticity.

Dr. Dick and his fishing partner, the renowned fish con-servationist Roger Bachman, bought the Fitzpatrick place forty-five years ago for a few thousand dollars. God only knows what it's worth now, given its location three miles up-stream from the locked gate that signals the territorial edge of the Deschutes Club, one of the most exclusive old fishing so-cieties in the world.

Founded in 1934, the Deschutes Club maintained a strict, male-only membership of fifty until 1996, when daughters were allowed to inherit a membership. As Guido, who is not a member, puts it, "The waiting list to get in is seventy years long." But club members themselves aren't snobbish, he in-sists, they're just lucky. "They're just a bunch of fishing fa-natics from Portland who happened to stumble onto the best dry-fly fishing stream in North America back when going to the Deschutes was like going to Siberia."

The club claims about fifteen miles of private water on the east side of the river. This quiet, underpopulated fishing heaven starts just past the locked gate some seven miles up-stream from the desert outpost of Maupin, then ends at a spot called North Junction. Anyone can float through it and fish it from a boat or raft, or pull over and wade, but only members can drive in and fish from its banks. Nonmembers may fish eastside club water only as the guest of a member, which is why Guido and his friends still invite Len Dick over for din-ner, despite the terrible toll it takes on their cigar supply.

The site of these raucous repasts is Guido's family fishing retreat on the Deschutes' west bank, just a few miles upstream from Dr. Dick's place, compared to which it rates as a palace if only for having indoor plumbing. The Rahrs' river home is, in fact, part of a nine-house settlement called "Dant" after the Dant and Russell Mining Company, a now-defunct perlite extraction outfit that built the houses for its employees.

Dant is a strange little neighborhood, sitting out there in the middle of that sagebrush and basalt wilderness. Tall imported elm and sycamores shade the green lawns that reach east toward the river from each front door. Flowers bloom beneath windows in the spring and summer, and a sweet little frontage path links them all. Dant looks for all the world like a piece of a midwestern town hurled westward, intact and unharmed, by some tremendous tornado—with one exception: an intensity of purpose that glitters in the air there like danger.

People come to Dant for one reason—to fish. Nobody bakes each other pies, then stops by to chat. Look carefully and you'll see that nobody really cares too much about the gardens, either. Or housekeeping. Their focus is acutely ichthyological, their senses turned always toward the river. And woe be it to any neophyte angler who stops by to "talk fishing" uninvited, because like all great fishing streams the Deschutes is a river of secrets.

The string of abandoned houses at Dant was discovered in the early fifties by Guido's maternal grandfather, Thomas B. Malarkey, and his fishing pals. Malarkey's own grandfather had homesteaded in Maupin in the late 1800s, and rumor has it that Malarkey junior had grown up fishing the Deschutes with him. Guido's rascally granddad remains one of the Deschutes Club's legendary fishermen, and still holds the club record for steelhead—forty-three hooked in one year. He caught his last one at the age of eighty-four, and died in 1993 at the age of ninety-two without telling Guido the location of his secret steelhead holes on the club side of the river. But in the end he told Len Dick. And we were about to fish one of them.

"This is the Smart House Riffle," Dr. Dick announced. His new red Jeep bounced so badly in the potholes I thought he had lapsed into one of the African dialects he'd learned as a missionary doctor in Kenya. Just to be sporting I answered him in French, but the good doctor ignored me and turned off the terrible gravel road that fronts Deschutes Club water and onto what looked like a dirt cow path.

"This is great nymphing water," Len Dick declared. "And dry-fly water, which is often one and the same."

Nymphs. One of the anchors of the fly fishing lexicon. Funny how the word spoken falls ever on the angler's ear like a bungled cast, that even erudite fishermen are reduced to Sylvester the Cat–status when ere they pronounce its sputtering single syllable: nymphs. Interesting how such a non–onomatopoeic word should inspire mental images of a glamorous, bewadered subspecies of the infamous *Starletta hollywoodae* in the minds of every aspiring male fly fisherman. While it is true that in Latin, Virgil defined *nymphae,* a first-declension feminine plural noun, as "half-divine beings believed to inhabit the seas, streams and woods," in this case you boys would be well advised to move farther on down the food chain. A lot farther. All the way to insect larva. Because that's precisely what a nymph is, and that's what nymph flies imitate. And know them we must, since nymphs make up the vast majority of a river fish's diet, a fact that illustrates why male and female anglers alike are obliged to become amateur entomologists. Like it or not, when you take up fly fishing, you take up bug collecting, which explains why I once happened upon an elderly gentleman-angler standing at the river's edge wiggling around in his waders singing:

"Do the Bug-Bug-Bug-Bug-Bug-Bug-Bug-Bug Boogie! Do-the-Bug, do-the-Bug, do-the-Bug, do-the-Bug Boogie!"

Then again, maybe it doesn't explain it. It does, however, tell us why Dr. Dick pulled a length of icky-looking wire screen attached to two beat-up blocks of wood out of the back of his car and proceeded to plunge it into the shallows alongside the Smart House Riffle.

"Oh, look at that! Isn't she beautiful!"

The doctor stared merrily into the screen of his home-made bug catcher. We were, I had been instructed, "seining for invertebrates," a preparatory ritual that gives fly fishermen a fish-eye glimpse into the current fauna of the current. Standing in several feet of water, and leaning precariously upon a hazelnut-wood walking staff that made him look like an octogenarian pole-vaulter, Dr. Dick had filtered about five minutes' worth of rushing river. Lifting his seine with the delicacy of a lover, he had then turned his attention to its wriggling green elephant-sneeze of a "take" with a rapture that can only be called bug love.

"Now, see that double claw? That means she's a mayfly nymph," Dr. Dick announced. "No, wait a minute . . . it means she's a stonefly . . . oh, I always get those mixed up."

He put a damp hand on his furrowed brow, rolled his eastern-bluebird eyes heavenward, and recited out loud: "A mayfly nymph has gills on its abdomen, and a stonefly nymph does not. So, a mayfly has a single claw and a stonefly has a double. That's it. All right, my girl, what we've got here is indeed a mayfly nymph—dammit, I mean a stonefly."

To me it looked more like Darth Vader after a recent trip to New Guinea. Black, shrunken, and hard-shelled, the little half-inch monster clung to the doctor's fingertip with gruesome desperation. So that is a genuine stonefly nymph, I thought. Yuck.

When you study the entomological fundamentals of fly fishing in the sport's many how-to books, the Bug Big Three—stonefly, mayfly, and caddis—take on mythic qualities. You imagine them gallant and winged, prehistoric and important, and reckon that when you finally see your first one in the wild the experience will offer up a shock of recognition akin to, say, setting foot in China for the first time ("There really *is* a China!"). Or shaking hands with the President ("He really *is* sexy!"). Or buying your first Mont Blanc pen ("It really *does* leak on airplanes!"). One does not expect to be grossed out. At least, I thought, this makes fishing with pretty, feathery, fake flies a lot more appealing than trying to stick a hook through a piece of living primordial weirdness.

Dr. Dick dipped his seine into the Deschutes once more, waited a few minutes, then continued his invertebrate inventory.

"Oh, oh. Look! Come here, you little rascal. Now *this* is a caddis—see the green on him? We also call him a green rock worm. He's a free-living caddis larva—doesn't make a case."

"The case against a case?" I offered, but Dr. Dick ignored me.

"And, oh! I think we've got a mayfly nymph," he announced. "See her yellow belly? No, I see a double claw. It's another stonefly."

Hoping for a mayfly, Dr. Dick made a third pass with his now hopelessly gooped-up seine.

"Ho-ho-ho!" he cried finally. "What have we got here?"

From the depths of his fly vest, Dr. Dick retrieved an antique, tortoiseshell-rimmed magnifying glass that had belonged to his mother, then proceeded to press it against an uncommonly small dark bug.

"I think it is a mayfly!" he concluded happily. "And there's another green rock worm." Dr. Dick stooped and turned over a rock. "Aha! And a bunch of caddis cocoons, too," he proclaimed. "Now, other flies don't build cocoons until they're ready to sprout wings, but a caddis builds a cocoon right away—see how he lines it with little rocks?"

I did see, but I could hardly believe what I saw. There, resting in Dr. Dick's palm, was a miniature masterpiece of subaquatic camouflage. Short, dark, and about the size of a baby monkey's baby finger, the little caddis larva's case was festooned with a dazzling array of tiny pebbles. They looked like Fred Flintstone's cigars, freeze-dried and stashed in the river away from Dr. Dick's watchful eye. He had, of course, found them anyway.

I was flummoxed. Does the caddis worm-thing build its cocoon first, then wiggle around sticking rocks on it like a pupa Picasso before it permanently seals itself inside? Or does it seal itself inside, then roll around blind on the river bottom like Ray Charles in a mummy bag, and hope for the best?

"I haven't the slightest idea," Dr. Dick replied irritably. Clearly, he had all the information he needed: we would fish nymphs.

"Now, this is a pheasant-tail nymph," he announced. "We're tying our fly on with a Turle knot. When you get to be eighty, you rely on your old knots because that's all you remember. And we'll start with a fluorescent orange strike indicator because nymphs are wet flies and that means they fish underwater, and that means we can't see 'em or see when a fish takes 'em, so we use a strike indicator which floats on the surface and we watch that."

The day had warmed and the early lavender light had brightened to a midday glare. The spent grasses of autumn had turned the hills to buckskin, ornamented here and there with golden beads of autumn alders, green beads of oak. It was my second day on the Deschutes, and already the place had revealed itself as a theater-in-the-round. By choosing a point of unspoiled earth and staying put, you bear witness to nature's ever-changing dramas. Moment by moment, season by season, the elements alter and adjust, and you are privy not just to sunset at the end of a day indoors, but to the entire waking process as the light moves along the color wheel and the zephyrs rise and fall and rise again, and something dies and the buzzards find it, and something is born and leaves its mother's

body to join the Great Play, and a nymph, after the long dor-
mant years, shifts in its husk and shimmies to the river's surface to split its final nymphal case and rise bewinged and free
into the sweet desert air. Or, just as often, into the waiting
mouth of a hungry trout. Tragedy? Comedy? Pathos? Or just
the simple complicated way of things. Whatever, you settle
deeply into a kind of mind-cocoon sometime during the second day on a river, and you stop worrying about the petty details of your own life. No wonder harried modern folk so love
fly fishing; I myself was already considering reconsidering my
rigid, ocean-only definition of home. No wonder Izaak
Walton pronounced fly fishing the one true western meditation. "God spare us from meditations," Annie Dillard once
wrote. When I heard her speak in Seattle years later, someone
in the audience asked her if she still felt as close to God as she
had when she wrote *Pilgrim at Tinker Creek*. Without missing
a beat, Annie spat back: "Well, what happened to *you* in the
last twenty years?" Someone should take the woman fishing.

"Someone should teach you to fish," Dr. Dick hissed.
Grabbing my casting hand with his, he drew back my rod and
gave it a startling thwack forward.

"Most people want to throw the line, but"—thwack!—
"it's a jerk. Remember, a fly rod is half a bow-and-arrow. If
you want to shoot it, you have to load it. So jerk! Jerk! Jerk!
That's better. Okay, get your wading staff, kid, we're moving
on," and he went sloshing off in the opposite direction from
where we'd parked.

Gentleman that he is, Dr. Dick had earlier fashioned me
an alpenstock out of a downed alder branch, so he wouldn't
have to watch his pupil wash downstream with the rest of the

river's flotsam. He had a point: my unschooled feet were about as river-proof as his eighty-year-old knees, so I welcomed the aid of this wooden extra leg. It did slow me down, though, so Dr. Dick was many yards upstream before I caught up with him and delicately suggested that we head *toward* his Jeep.

~~~~~

"All right, we're going to drive an hour downriver and I'm going to need two rubbers and some wooden doweling."

It is unnerving to hear this sort of announcement from an eighty-year-old man with his fly down, while being held captive in the front seat of a new red Laredo Jeep. The only response I could think of was "You *do*?"

"Yes, I need them for my rod," Dr. Dick replied coolly. "But an inner tube would do just as well."

"It *would*?"

"Yes, and mountain-bike inner tubes are the best."

"They *are*?"

Without warning, Dr. Dick suddenly climbed out of his Jeep, but to my relief he began rummaging around in the back seat.

"Aha, my girl!" he said finally. "Hallelujah, we're saved! Buy Jesus a beer, he must be tired of all that religion!"

Saved from what, I wanted to know.

"From having to listen to our fishing rods rattle around on the roof rack for an hour, that's what."

As it turned out, Dr. Dick has an ingenious way of affixing his equipment to the top of his car that involves looping a thick, homemade rubber band around the end of each rod and pinioning it with a few inches of doweling. It's a Third

World sort of solution, one of those thrifty, self-reliant, highly effective practices that will surely leave the planet when the last person who lived through the Great Depression does.

So we drove along in relative peace, spared from external clatter, anyway, but certainly not from Dr. Dick's stream-of-consciousness brand of conversation. He is something of a semantic gazelle, able to leap from critical analysis ("Joan Wulff's stuff is so complicated I can't understand half of it!") to biological alchemy ("Now, when a mayfly gets out of his nymphal shuck, he dries off his wings for a few seconds, then becomes a dun.") to the proper design of walking staffs ("The reason I like hazelnut wood is that it's light and you can't break it. Guido's dad said all the alpenstocks in Austria are out of hazelnut wood—I thought I discovered it!") without the slightest indication of mental whiplash. His lack of self-editing has mortified many a family member. He once informed a friend that she'd look much prettier in photographs if she'd stop dyeing her hair, to which she replied curtly: "If you had been my physician, you would know the depth of the inaccuracy of your assumption."

But since Dr. Dick is a master of the nonstop blurted statement, he asks no questions and expects no response; thus his endless monologue makes for pleasant background noise, and it allowed my own mind to roam the scenery.

In the later light the canyon's basaltic ridges loomed muscular and terse, lost both to the newborn delicacy of dawn and the feminine sensuality of morning. By evening they would cower and bend and dissolve again into the shadows—their changing presence like a life lived wholly in one day.

I regarded their high, hawk-colored shoulders, considered
their mass and unfathomable weight, and was struck most by
the power not of rock, but of water.

It took three and a half million years for the Deschutes to
claim its place here, to lay down a line and follow it to the
end. Its work was not without interruptions. Like everything
else on the western edge of the continent, the Deschutes
Canyon sits squarely upon the Ring of Fire. Over the mil-
lennium, the demon gods of the neighborhood volcanoes
pitched one unholy fit after another, their hot lava roadblocks
making the river change directions more often than Dr. Dick.
At one point they threw a whole mountain range in its path,
blocking its original route west to the Pacific and sending it
forever north to the Columbia. It had to go. It had no choice.
So year after year, century after century, the water bore down
on the rock, licking at labradorite, picking at pyroxene, and
etching into it all an uncanny likeness of itself. The canyon
bottom took on the exact shape of the river, the river made
it its own. For all the loud theatrics of the rock, water won.

There, in the steady trickle of Dr. Dick's verbal down-
pour, I decided to go at this irksome business of learning to
cast the way the river went at the rock. And let it take as long
as it took.

I remember the rest of that day as one long casting lesson
delivered in classic Deschutes car-fishing style: drive five minutes, stop, fish until Dr. Dick pronounced that we'd "caught
all the fish in this spot" (which was to say none), and drive
again. I seem to remember more trees—maybe because as my
casting became bolder I caught more.

"Fish don't live in trees," Dr. Dick informed me several

times in exactly the same tone Walter Cronkite used to use for reports on Vietnam.

We had switched to dry flies, mostly, I think, for my benefit: you can see them. Our dry flies were supposed to imitate mayfly "spinners," or mature, flying mayflies that only moments before, as I understood it, were "duns," which were weak, not fully formed, winged insects that until very recently had been nymphs.

"So, what do wet flies imitate?" I asked.

"A drowned spinner," Dr. Dick replied without taking his eyes off the river. "Or a dun that hasn't flown yet. But mostly nymphs."

"So duns and dead spinners don't float?"

"Oh, sometimes they do," Dr. Dick said testily, "but the way you're casting, the fish aren't going to pay any attention anyway."

Len broke off my now sopping-wet "dry fly" and tied on a hare's-ear nymph, guaranteed to imitate a mayfly nymph. The idea was to sink the fly to the fish and swing it by them enticingly.

When I finally did manage to make my fly land halfway near a decent piece of water, Dr. Dick would yell: "Mend it!" At first I thought he thought my cast was so bad he wanted me to redo the whole thing.

"No," he said, grabbing my rod, "I mean mend it." And he gave it a little Merlin's-magic-wand loopty-loop, a lifting gesture that raised the belly of my line out of its downstream bulge and straightened it out on higher water. Fascinating, I thought. "Keeps the fly out in the current," Dr. Dick concluded. He made a second mend, then a third, "then you lead it in," he said, describing the graceful arc in which the current pulls one's line at the end of a good drift. I was beginning to get the picture. Not a nanosecond after my first confident angling thought, a fish hit my fly.

"Oh, God!" I breathed.

"God had nothing to do with it," Dr. Dick replied. "Lenox is here."

I played the fish for maybe three seconds, then it was gone. But, as with Guido's fish the day before, the electricity of connection remained. My hands were shaking. I cast again. This time my line landed on the water in a bundled mess instead of a straight line, and I started to redo it.

"Leave it!" Dr. Dick commanded. "Anytime the fly hits the water, you leave it."

I left it, and got another strike.

"That wasn't a strike," he assured me. "That was a rock. You got a rock fish."

Our last stop was a pretty little riffle, backdropped by the thickest riparian vegetation we'd seen so far.

"All right, time for Len Dick's Change-of-Direction," the Duke of Dyslexia declared. I thought that we'd already gone over that one.

"Don't be smart. It's a cast. In fact, it's the best one for this kind of situation. Now, instead of making a back-cast, you'll false-cast to the right. Then, letting out more line, to the left, then finally cast upstream to the right again."

He meant to say false-cast to the left, then to the right, and finally to the left again, which was, in fact, upstream, but I didn't say anything. After all, I myself am directionally dyslexic and am hopeful that it's a sign of creativity. I was

about to relate this to Dr. Dick but, once again, he had
grabbed my fishing hand and was busy punching my fly rod
violently into the air, this time to my left, right, and left.

"Now, shoot it!" he cried, and miracle of miracles, my
line indeed shot upstream straight and true. It was my best
cast of the day.

"Len Dick's Change-of-Direction," my modest coach intoned. "Works every time."

I know some lucky ones come by angling naturally, but
not I. Perhaps it was the dearth of childhood sports available
to the women of my generation. Perhaps it's my natural lack
of upper-body strength despite my one-cast success. Maybe
my moon is just always in klutz. Whatever it was, my borrowed fly rod continued to feel like a lightning bolt with a
mind of its own, the river continued to overwhelm me, and
I continued to walk in it like the Dork of the Deschutes.

In my own defense, I am a person who learns by repetition. I could not, for instance, pronounce the French "r"
when I arrived in Provence to spend my junior year abroad.
Try as I might, I gargled every r-word into oblivion, much to
the disgust of teacher and waiter alike. Then, six months later
to the day, I woke up in the morning and could do it. Even
throat-grabbers like *revers* (reverse) and *grenouille* (frog) and—
sacré bleu!—*murmurer* (murmur) were no match for the likes
of *moi*. I could do it and that was that. Now I could only pray
that one mysterious day, after practice as steadfast as water on
rock, my luck would *revers* and my line would suddenly sail
through the cool river air like the tongue of a *grenouille*,
drawing many a hushed *murmurer* from my unsuspecting fishing coach. It would also finally gain me entry into the only

secret society I'd ever wanted desperately to join—the greater club of fly fishing whose members know that the fastest path to enlightenment is to see the world as one long fishing trip.

"The motto of every serious angler is 'Nearer My God to Thee,'" writes Tom McGuane in his book of fishing essays, *Live Water*. It seemed easy enough with Dr. Dick serving as my self-nominated god. While he spoke endlessly of other things during the drive back, his casting commands rang endlessly in my head.

"Mend it!"

"Leave it!"

And always . . .

"Punch it, dammit! Punch it. It's *not* in the wrist!"

For some reason his commands made me think of my father. But unlike Dr. Dick, Daddy was quiet when he drove—unless the urge to sing overtook him, in which case my sister and I prayed for silence. In fact, I can hardly remember a thing my father said. As the sky above the canyon bruised and darkened, the old pain began to spread in my chest. I missed him. No, I realized, I missed the father I wanted him to have been. So many of us do. For sons, paternal neglect damages who they are to themselves. For daughters, I think it limits a sense of our value to the opposite sex, our belief in our own lovability.

But these were, by now, old ideas—things I thought I'd worked through years earlier, so I wondered what it was about Dr. Dick that had brought them forth again. I considered this for a moment, then decided that maybe there's not much difference between someone who makes one impersonal announcement after another, and someone who says nothing at all. The end product is the same: disconnection.

The day quickened, the light fell, and soon we were back at Dr. Dick's place. He had rowed us across the river at twilight, and now the night was so black, the stars so far-flung, it looked as though the soul of every fish ever killed by a fisherman had ganged up to glare down at us from the heavens. Still, I was grateful to be alive and warm there in the old Fitzpatrick homestead. Dr. Dick had made a good fire in the woodstove and had water on for tea. He fiddled around in the kitchen, making me toast and digging out butter and somebody's homemade jam and someone else's unbelievably good chocolate-chip cookies.

"Who *made* these?" I sang.

"Oh, Helene, my wife. She does everything. Even cuts my hair."

I nearly choked.

"Except she was too busy last week, so I went to a barber and he just butchered the hell out of it."

Mightily relieved, I swallowed.

In this homey setting Dr. Dick's conversation took a turn toward the domestic. On his many trips to and from the table, he seemed to shift into his old nurturing physician role and questioned me nonstop on my home life, my husband, my problematic marriage; then he offered unflinching counsel.

"You're a sophisticated nature girl," he proclaimed. "You need a nature boy with a literary mind. A city boy with a sports mind will never do. Now, Helene, she couldn't care less about fishing, but, oh, she loves the hunt. Hikes all up and down those hills. Can hit anything."

"I bet she can cook anything, too," I said.

"Oh, Helene's a great cook."

And so it went, our little end-of-the-day conversation. I confess I can't recall having an older gentleman so genuinely interested in the details of my small life. Dr. Dick's concern was fatherly, really, and I was quite touched by it.

"You know," I said finally, "I think everyone's got you wrong. I don't think you're a curmudgeon at all. In fact, I think you're very sweet."

At that, Dr. Dick whirled around midstep, fixed me with his aristocratic glacial gaze, and said: "Don't be a fool. You're a young, pretty woman, otherwise I wouldn't be doing any of this."

Chapter Four

THE BLUE HOUR

Dinner at Dant is a thing of beauty, if you consider exalted debauchery beautiful, and dinner that night was no exception. While I had been under Dr. Dick's tutelage, Guido
had shaken a hatchery steelhead from the river, and others
had plucked a peck of Asian partridges from the high ridges.
The scent of barbecued fish swam on the chilled autumn air,
adding a sweet note to the blunt perfume of oven-roasting
chukar.

As I worked on preparing a Brazilian chocolate cake,
friends leaned against the kitchen doorjamb, merrily holding
forth on all manner of theory and science, their cheeks as red
as their wine, their eyes broadcasting the dazzling light that re-
places the haze of the city after just one day on the water. I

knew only one thing could make me happier: learning to cast.

I thought about it while pretending to listen to the lively discourse around me. I thought about it while measuring flour. I even raised my mixing spoon in an unconscious rehearsal, rocking it high in the air beside my right ear, splattering my hair and the walls with troutlike spots. As I did, Dr. Dick's earlier counsel drowned out even the current Dant chorus: "It's not like swinging a hammer or throwing a ball. Your fly rod is a new tool that requires a motion you haven't used before."

That new motion—not to mention my new hairdo—was the sticky wicket. And I didn't know if it was a rhythm thing or a timing thing, a muscle-control issue or a memory problem. Maybe it was a grip thing—I couldn't tell. All I knew is that when I tried to "load the rod" like "half a bow-and-arrow," keeping it airborne "between one and eleven o'clock," my line ended up laying itself down on the water with all the linearity of a wild boar's tusk. It was *that* savage, *that* dangerous, and *that* . . . curly. Accuracy was out of the question; in fact, my line wasn't even in the same zip code.

So how does one master the art of wagging a fly rod back and forth? It couldn't be a rhythm thing, I thought, because if there's one thing I've got, it's rhythm—my mother didn't win the University of Texas jitterbug contest for nothing. And timing? Well, that could be problematic, but my timing deficiencies usually show up in joke delivery, not physical acts where rhythm can see me through. Muscle control might be the culprit, but then Dr. Dick kept telling me that casting is about finesse, not brute force. Memory defects were a defi-

nite possibility—I still couldn't remember how to attach my
reel to my rod, much less all of Guido's and Dr. Dick's rules
and regulations. And the grip seemed like a no-brainer. "You
can grip the rod handle at either end, or in the middle," Dr.
Dick had assured me. "It doesn't matter."

Despite all the variables and advice, like love and marriage it seemed to me that learning to cast ought to be a lot
easier than it was. I couldn't shake the feeling that something
was missing, some specific key ingredient, some little basic
something that everyone had overlooked. But what, besides
months of practice, could it be?

I thought about it all through dinner, which was sublime,
and on through the night's fourth and fifth bottles of wine. I
thought about it during several toasts of somebody's excellent
port, and through rave reviews for my cake, though, by then,
heated Twinkies would have drawn a standing ovation from
that crowd. When Guido finally led his guests over the edge
of the Excess Abyss by cracking open a bottle of Wild Turkey,
I retired to my room and thought about casting from the
depths of my sleeping bag.

I woke up thinking about it, and continued to do so the
next morning as fellow Dantites emerged from their respective places of repose, bilious, squinting, and Frankenstein-
walking into the kitchen, seeking coffee. I thought about it
while Guido poured himself a bowl of Lucky Charms, put
the bowl up to his face, and ate them dry, like a stupefied
horse. For a moment I thought about how everyone's skin
was the same color as the green charms he was chomping,
then I got back to thinking about casting. Why, I wanted to

know, was it so impossible for me to control a fly rod? Why was it so difficult to learn something completely new?

I was still thinking about it when I headed home later that day. The question so obsessed me that I decided not to head for home at all, and turned south instead to visit my mother, who lives near Eugene, Oregon, and is a psychologist with special knowledge of the mysterious ways of the brain. If anyone could answer my questions, she could. But Eugene was still two hours away, so I continued my contemplation of the angling learning curve, my thoughts arriving now like mental storyboards telling tales of human will and triumph.

First I saw a baby. Clinging to a sofa arm. Wobbling like a drunk. Intoxicated with desire to take her first step. Willing to fall in order to walk. Grinning like the Buddha.

Then I saw a boy. Smooth, long muscle flexing beneath cinnamon skin. Hurling a sphere twice as big as his head toward a basket-in-the-sky. Air ball. Throws again. Nothing. Again. It sails through. Dumb luck? Progress? Like a Holy Roller fixated on the hereafter, the child never takes his eyes off his own circle of heaven.

Finally, a teenage girl. Bonnie Raitt look-alike. Can't leave her brother's guitar alone. Walking blues. Her fingers strut. Holds the same high notes over and over. Sounds like a catfight to her mother. Can't she do something else? No. She can't. It would be like trying to stop the falling rain, or standing in the track of a runaway train.

Every day somebody somewhere becomes obsessed with an idea that won't turn them loose. Something new. Something they just have to do. At age eighty, political analyst I. F.

Stone decided to learn Greek just to prove he could do it. He did. At age seventy-two, my own mother suddenly took up watercolors. She knew nothing about painting. Had never painted in her life. Yet the greenhouse was converted into an art studio, books were purchased, supplies ordered, any watercolor class offered within a hundred-mile radius signed up for, and she spent every waking moment trying to make her new brushes and colors work.

Her early efforts didn't exactly exude talent. There were a lot of falls and air balls, even catfights—when she literally threw herself down on her studio floor and wailed. But she continued, stroke by unsure stroke, painting one garden flower after another until grace finally crept into each petal, and each blossom bloomed with a colorful luminescence. Her progress stunned everyone in the family, as well as her new-found artist friends who had been painting for decades.

After only a year and a half, my mother was invited to exhibit her work in the annual Valley River Art Show, held each October in Eugene's Valley River Shopping Center, about twenty miles downstream from where she and my stepfather now live on the McKenzie River. So I stopped by to see her latest works, and to assail her brain with brainy questions.

"So, what happens to our brain," I asked her, there in the shopping mall, "when we try to do something we've never done before?" I had almost said, "when we wear hats like that," because for some reason my mother was wearing a wide-brimmed chapeau garnished with garish artificial flowers. This was most uncharacteristic. In fact, I had walked right past her, thinking to myself, "God, I'm glad *my* mother doesn't wear stupid hats like that." Now I was having trouble conjuring up my usual respect for her extensive knowledge of the brain in all its glory.

"Well," she nodded, shifting into her professorial voice, which made the hat look even more inane, "even before a baby is born there are physical neuropathways in its brain made out of noncognitive brain tissue. Actually, they're called phantom pathways, because they're just little fluid empty spaces where brain cells can grow—what we call grey matter."

"Like streambeds?" I ventured, trying to avoid the hypnotic power of her gigantic wagging hat-rose.

"Yes, you could say that. Now, all of us are born with ten billion brain cells to the eleventh power, plus or minus one . . ."

(Definitely minus, I thought.)

" . . . and even the most intelligent human beings have only developed ten percent of those. Some of those brain cells are predesignated to do certain jobs—to become vision cells, or hearing cells. Some will make the baby walk."

(And some will make us buy hats that make us look like Minnie-Pearl-Goes-to-Paris.)

"Now, when an adult human learns anything new, undeveloped brain cells are stimulated to grow along the edges of undeveloped neuropathways, thickening their sides and making them deeper."

"Like rivers?" I asked, relieved to return to familiar territory.

"Yes, all right, like rivers. Then the new pathways make other new pathways that connect in many places . . . like tributaries."

"So," I said, "let's say that I'm trying to consistently move a fly rod between ten or eleven o'clock and one o'clock, keeping my elbow tight against my side and my eye on a particular spot in the river while trying not to get knocked over by the current."

"Then you're going to fall in," she laughed, "because your brain needs to make new connections between the brain cells that control your hand muscles and the ones that control your arm muscles and your leg muscles and your vision. We can only guess," my mother continued, "but we probably experience what we call 'breakthroughs' when these new connections are complete and available for use. And if you quit, of course, the connections weaken. But if you begin practicing again, they get stronger faster, and no one can explain that. The phenomenon is called 'Learning to Ice Skate in the Summer.'"

I was a lot more interested in learning to fly fish in the fall. "Mother," I whined, "I'm *really* having a hard time with this. I mean, I cast and cast and cast, and the line is supposed to shoot out straight, but mine either comes out all curled up or lands with a big splash that would terrify any fish. Then every once in a while I magically make a perfect cast, but I don't have a clue how I did it, and the next one is all messed up again." (My voice was starting to take on howler-monkey qualities.) "And when I watch Guido or Dr. Dick cast," I shrieked, "it's like the rod is part of their *body*—like another *arm* or something—they're so graceful and their line just lays down on the water *perfectly* straight every time. But *my* rod feels like a UFO that just whips all over the place. I can't even imagine controlling it like they do, and I'm just *so* frustrated! *How do they do it?*"

My mother shrugged. "The banks of their fly fishing neuropathway rivers have been built up for decades. You just don't have any brain cells . . . there."

I sighed. "Okay, so let me get this straight: when I practice casting, my brain is actually building thicker banks along streambeds in my head that will turn into rivers that eventually will connect with other rivers, so that finally, one day, I won't feel like I have water on the brain when I fish?"

"That's right, and remember, ninety percent of the neocortex—the new brain—is given to vision, so although people often think of fishing as a dumb sport, fly fishing may actually require the highest cooperation of the brain cells."

The highest cooperation of brain cells. The idea swam around in my head like bait-tank sardines during the entire five-hour drive back to my home on the island. By the time I arrived at the ferry dock, I figured at least several of my brain cells were cooperating more fully. Fortunately, so were the weather gods. It had rained all the way from Eugene to Olympia—big winter-is-coming tears that splashed on the road and created their own microfog. Then, about a half-hour after that, the heavens suddenly cleared, the sky went pink, and half a dozen long flat Northwest clouds lay themselves down like gold ribbons across the box of sky in my windshield, the gift of a fine autumn day.

Hope lived in that topaz light. I stopped at a roadside farm and bought pumpkins and Indian corn, then arranged them on the passenger seat with the desert sage I'd taken at the Deschutes Club gate, a sweet little shrine to seasonal materialism. Would that I could have laid down my first steelhead there, too.

The ferry pulled itself quietly across Puget Sound toward my little green island while a dozen cormorants stood drying themselves open-winged and motionless atop pilings nearby.

"I have made a terrible mistake," I announced in the cooling evening air. "Fly fishing is not a battle, yet I have been at war with the rod!"

I was right. Every time I had tried to cast, my anger at my own ineptitude had transferred directly to my fly rod. But why was I angry in the first place? I knew I was a rookie, so why did I have such a hard time being a crummy caster? And why was it so hard for me to keep practicing without instant progress?

Then I remembered the core message of one of my favorite self-improvement books, George Leonard's *Mastery:* to take the master's journey you have to practice diligently . . . to keep practicing even when you seem to be getting nowhere.

So why can't I just accept that I'm getting nowhere?

Maybe, I mused, it's because my family was *so* goal-oriented. My father wasn't, really, but my mother always has been, and so has my stepfather. My mother divorced my father when I was five and my sister Valerie almost four. Three years later she married our stepfather, Robert Meeker, and they had our sister Heather. Both Mother and Bob went on to earn their Ph.D.s and create a remarkably successful educational research institute. So, I reasoned, if only by example, my sisters and I were raised in an achievement-oriented environment with endless support for whatever it was we wanted to do. Success wasn't so much expected as it was assumed. Maybe, then, I was confusing the rookie's reality with failure. Or maybe I was just plateau-phobic.

The plateau is the flat, redundant Place of Practice, the Arena of Attempt, the personal workout Stadium of the Seeker who hopes to hit a 250-yard three-wood onto the green, or read the Upanishads in the original Sanskrit . . . or, God help us, cast a fly line properly. But the American mind has been raised on the sensational, not the nice water-on-rock pace of the plateau. Coat it with a ganache of Cajun rhythm, Scottish gung-ho, and general familial ambition, and it's no wonder life on the plateau drove me crazy.

It was time for an attitude adjustment of monumental proportions. Because, if you think about it, it's obvious that we're all going to spend about 99.9 percent of our time on the plateau. So, rather than think of the plateau as the Oakland of the student's journey, a boring, there-less nowhere that simply must be endured, why not think of it as the Disneyland of the Disciples, where Goofy is king, Mickey Mouse calls the shots, and the only way to make any real progress is if Tinkerbell happens to spill fairy dust on you.

George Leonard couldn't agree more. "It's simple," he concludes. "To be a learner, you've got to be willing to be a fool."

~~~~~

"OK, Tillie, here's the drill. I'm going to stand here and make this long stick go back and forth about four million times and you're going to chase birds."

I have never seen a dog who likes to chase birds as much as my dog Tillie does. Her enthusiasm was just what I needed, and, besides, I hadn't seen her for days. So after the ferry deposited me onto the island, I swung by the house, picked Tillie up, and as the day headed for the last quarter we headed for the nearest beach.

Being a Welsh corgi, Tillie has five-inch legs and a three-inch clearance, but she will take on the craftiest crow, the swiftest swallow, with an energy that verges on the heroic, tracking their aerial path from twenty feet below, running full-speed-ahead, a hairy little piglet on No-Doz. So while she sprinted up and down the sand, ruffling buffleheads and giving the grebes grief, I waded into Puget Sound and attempted to make peace with Guido's 6-weight Winston, which he had loaned me on the condition that I "use it or lose it." As always, it felt like putty in my hands, Merlin's magic wand whose password I still knew not: I really *did* feel like Mickey Mouse.

But I kept on casting, over and over and over again, against the failing sky. I turned to witness each back-cast, just as Guido had taught me to. I waited the extra beat Dr. Dick insisted on before I tried to "punch" it forward as was his command. I felt graceless, a rusty robot moving its metallic arm in unoiled jerks and starts. Worse, I felt like a spectacle, as though standing out on an open beach invited both observation and assessment—surely half a dozen living-room telescopes were trained my way, their owners' scoffs spicing up the family dinner hour.

As the light died and fell, mercifully, so did my wretched self-consciousness. Egos are restless devils, and if you can ignore their demands for attention long enough, they eventually leave you alone. Evidently casting practice bores the hell out of mine. Maybe thirty minutes into it, the thought occurred to me that I hadn't thought about myself for quite a while. In fact, I hadn't had a thought of any sort for quite a while. It was similar to realizing that you've been driving for who knows how long with your mind completely elsewhere, and you don't have a clue about how you got to where you are, but things appear to be fine and there you are, on the road, driving. Or, in my case, casting.

The funny thing was that my casting *had* improved. It wasn't great, but it was more natural, smoother. Had a few more brain cells popped up along my neural streambed? If so, does that only happen when you're busy making other plans? I didn't feel fatigued, either. Actually I felt sort of . . . happy. Maybe, I thought, this is what George Leonard meant when he said that practice exists only in the present, and to love the plateau is to love the eternal now.

A clatter of croaking and barking drew my attention down the beach. I figured it was some dog-and-birdie show. It was. In the past I had watched Tillie chase a great blue heron out of the shallows, and even with its slow-motion flapping it outdistanced her in two seconds flat. She loved it. Every spring, nesting swallows dive-bomb her head and give her false hope, and she loves that. Corgis are a herding breed, and the fact that her bird herd is a good twenty feet off the ground never diverts her from her task. Perhaps Tillie's instincts are strong enough to override the laws of basic physics, or maybe that's inbreeding for you. Whatever. This time she'd run up against a covey of crows who, as writer David Quam-

men has pointed out, are too intelligent for their station and
are therefore given to pranks and tomfoolery to stave off certain boredom.

Sure enough, they were engaged in an elaborate chore-
ography clearly designed to torture my dear determined dog-
gie. One crow would light on a piece of driftwood and wait
until Tillie was nearly upon it, then lift off like a helicopter
while a second swooped in from behind to buzz her unsuspecting derriere. They literally had the poor girl turning in
circles.

She loved it. And dutifully chased each bird as it was presented to her without a thought of the futility of her actions.
Winning didn't seem to be part of her vocabulary, but practice sure was. A stunning concept began to form a little ball
in the back of my mind. Then it hit me: "Was Tillie . . . a
master?" She didn't care about *catching* a bird; the process of
trying to catch one was her only goal, and that kept her riv-
eted in the eternal now. Even her face was George Leonard's
description of the face of mastery, "relaxed and serene, sometimes faintly smiling." Tillie grinned the whole dang time!
She also quickly "settled into a steady, trancelike rhythm that
obliterated all considerations of time or repetition," and as the
crows had deftly shown, she was completely willing to play
the fool.

Come to think of it, so was my mother. In one breath-
taking moment I understood that she had practiced watercolors so long and hard, the boundaries between herself and her
art had blurred, and wearing that crazy hat at the art show
was simply her way of becoming the painting. Maybe this
chase game of Tillie's was her way of becoming the bird.

Should I figure out how to become the fish? Could *that* be the secret?

"Jeez," I thought as my dog's little form streaked by again, a low-flying comet against the blue hour of the approaching night, "maybe that's why dog is God spelled backwards."

Chapter Five

"I DON'T KNOW WHY I SWALLOWED THE FLY"

"As your fishing coach, I *insist* that you get your butt down here *now!*"

There is something about winter steelhead fishing that turns even the most eloquent fly fishermen into street hustlers. Maybe it's the cold call of the weather. Maybe it's the stealthiness of the fish. Maybe it's just that serious anglers have been cooped up indoors for the holidays too long. Hard to say. But nearly three months had elapsed since our last fishing trip, fall had fallen fully into the dark side of the year, and Guido knew it was time to get his comfort-loving apprentice out of the house. The edge in his voice told me I might as well dump my nice cup of hot tea down the drain, let the woodstove fire die out, and head for the impossibly soggy southwest corner of Washington State, even in the Neptunean month of January.

The quest for winter steelhead is the Iditarod of Northwest fly fishing. It is a demanding, ice-blooded, winter marathon that requires an unholy communion with the most merciless of meteorological elements: cold, rain, and wind. The climatic conditions of steelhead fishing are, in fact, what traditional Chinese medicine considers the most damaging to one's health: the invasion of damp cold. Chinese physicians also contend that most men naturally have a lot more blood and bioelectric energy—or *chi'i*—than women, which explains why nine out of ten couples fight over how high to set the car heater, and why women act like heat-seeking missiles in bed. This also explains why novice female anglers generally begin making hey-there's-a-really-neat-little-café-not-far-from-here noises after about three minutes on any winter steelhead river.

It does *not* explain, however, why a fishing coach would haul his rookie student into the heart of the fiercest fishing the Northwest has to offer.

"Because they're out there," Guido answered when I dared to ask. "And we're not."

"But winter steelheading is *impossible!*" I countered. "Even experts say so. And I still can't cast straight in perfect weather. How am I supposed to do it in a typhoon?"

"It'll be good practice," my coach replied in a voice like

frozen pond scum. "Don't wimp out on me, Max," he added, and hung up.

Steelhead season begins innocently enough in late fall when the maple leaves are still the color of the yellow line on the highway. Then you go because you know this chromium muscle of a fish has always been there and is there now, waiting in the watery lace, the bothered hem of the fast water in every coastal river and stream that still resembles itself.

This is festive fishing. Held forth in the heat of high harvest, when garden pumpkins still burn like planets beneath borrowed turquoise skies. And the clouds are round and fresh, gathering ever unto themselves like popping corn. And the leaves hover brightly in the air around deciduous trees, great fractured manes of persimmon and pomegranate, plum and gourd-yellow, all strobing wildly in the autumnal light. You know there will be salmon in the rivers, too. Times are rich.

Then it is winter. The sky waxes over and the rains fill the air with opals. There is no flaming foliage, no apples rubying the orchards, no elk in the rut. And the salmon—what's left of them—have long since become nutrients for their own rivers. It is winter and it is quiet and only the green arrows of the forest are left, pointing bravely to the laboring dawn.

Then you go in earnest. Because this silver silence, this drizzled, chilled elegance that turns fishing water to champagne and sends saner folk straight to their down comforters, *this* is the true season of the steelhead. In the Northwest it has always been this way. Guido was right; winter steelheading is a tradition, and whether I could cast or not, it was time to experience it.

"January, 1929, was a cold month on Vancouver Island." Thus does Roderick Haig-Brown begin the story of catching a twenty-two-pound steelhead in his fishing classic *A River Never Sleeps*. "Snow began drifting in coldly from the north, and the line kept freezing in the rings of the rod."

Oncorhynchus mykiss—the first word is Latin for "crooked beak," in honor of a steelhead's hooked snout; the second word is Russian for "rainbow trout," because steelhead are oceangoing rainbows (although the American Fisheries Society recently reclassified them as salmon). The Russians were the first to describe this trout species, which they discovered in a remote corner of the Kamchatka Peninsula. Steelhead remain one of the great anomalies of the North Pacific, and a Northwest angler's grandest prize, if only because they make you work so hard.

There are many reasons why steelhead are so tricky to catch. First of all, they're very, very wary. That's because they spend most of their time in the ocean dodging all manner of predators. Coastal steelhead, fresh in from the Pacific, are especially cagey. For instance, unlike salmon, they will not lie where they can be seen. For that reason they love boulder-strewn water that has a little riffle on top, so enemies can't see through it.

Furthermore, like all spawning fish, steelhead aren't feeding. But they're not territorial the way salmon are. Though spawning salmon aren't eating, either, it's a lot easier to get one to take a lure or fly; they attack it out of anger as a get-out-of-my-space move. Salmon are in the river for one reason: to spawn and die. Their decomposing bodies do their rivers the favor of fertilizing them with oceanic nutrients, an ancient synergistic relationship that is critical to the health of river ecosystems. Scientists have even identified marine carbon in old-growth trees. In fact, research in a Willapa Bay tributary has shown that up to 50 percent of the tissue in juvenile salmon and steelhead can be traced to the biomass of the previous year's salmon run.

Steelhead, on the other hand, spawn and then return to the ocean; their bodies do not undergo the kind of degeneration salmon bodies do. So a steelhead's instinct isn't full-court-press-anything-goes; it's programmed to survive, and remains, therefore, much more wary and sly than a salmon. (It's enlightening to note that it is mostly female steelhead—"hens"—that return to the ocean after spawning; males—"bucks"—generally hang around the spawning grounds until they've used up all their sperm in multiple fertilizations, and by then their bodies are too weak to survive the trip back.)

Another aspect of survival programming is basic spookiness. Steelhead are very spooky. They even spook easily when they're on their nests, or redds. "But when salmon are on their redds you've darn near got to step on them to move them," reports Cal Cole, one of Guido's colleagues at the Portland fish conservation organization Oregon Trout.

All in all, it's no surprise that it takes most fly fishermen years to land their first steelhead.

"That's the way steelhead fishing is; a great number of variable factors enter into it," Haig-Brown tells us, "and sure knowledge comes only from the hooking and killing of a fish and decently close observation of the place and conditions of the catch."

Steelhead are named for their exceptionally hard skulls. In fact, all of a steelhead's bones are thicker and heavier than a salmon's. Nonetheless, a steelhead is but a salmon wannabe.

If you look at a map of their range, you can guess why. Steelhead once ran the great arc from the coastal drainages of Kamchatka all the way around to Baja California. Now their strongest populations are on the west coast of the Kamchatka Peninsula and in southern Alaska, with the lion's share in British Columbia and a handful hanging on in Oregon and Washington. There the great rains dilute fluvial nutrients and deliver them directly into the Pacific. So what's a little fish to do if it wants to grow big and strong? Follow the food, of course. That's the theory, anyway, and ample proof doth dwell in the fact that an adult salmon or steelhead is far bigger than your average adult trout.

If they arrive in the spring or summer, they're considered summer-run steelhead. If they arrive between December and March, they're winter-run. On a map of their original range, steelhead streams literally marble the coasts of Washington and Oregon. Today, in the Lower 48, only six wild Pacific Northwest summer steelhead runs, or "stocks," are considered healthy, and only twenty-eight wild winter steelhead stocks are doing that well.

"And one of them is this one," Guido announced as his old blue VW van bullied its way through the vapor lock that separates southwestern Washington from the rest of the state. We were motoring slowly around the uterine lip of Willapa Bay, one of the most fecund estuaries left in the country. Nearly 1,500 miles of freshwater streams feed nutrients into the bay from the hills, and powerful tidal contractions flush its 88,000 liquid acres twice a day. On a map Willapa Bay does indeed look like a cross-sectioned womb, and well it should, for it is, after all, the mother-water to Dungeness crab, sturgeon, smelt, cutthroat trout, three species of salmon, seven species of clams, every sixth oyster consumed in the United States, and, yes, the wily wild steelhead.

It is a haunted landscape, the Willapa, with its dim mineral colors. Chronic rain-bashing bleaches them to phantoms of their former selves, then the thick lens of precipitation finishes them off. The gay raspberry of riparian willow goes a sickly mauve, the clear lime of eelgrass bleeds to celery, the mudflats lose their cocoa depth to a beige nothingness, the eye-blue of the bay blinks itself into a rheumy gauze, the sky suffers from total anemia, and even the rich hunter green of the firs falls back into a deathly puce ditch. Compared to the Willapa, the high desert palette of the Deschutes is positively vivacious. But it must be said: this saturated, holographic landscape is the perfect terrain for winter steelhead, the *arcanum arcanorum* of the fish kingdom.

"So, the secret of secrets," I sighed. "Why are steelhead so secretive, anyway?" The climate had exorcised any spirit from my voice. I felt like a clam and sounded, even to my own dulled ears, like a flounder.

"Because they're so cautious," Guido replied. His words dissipated into little clouds in front of his face.

"So, do they hide or something?"

"They hide and they're stealthy and they're on their way to their spawning grounds, so they're not feeding like a trout.

With classic steelheading, we tempt them with attractor patterns, something that just gets their attention instead of imitating a food item. But in the last few years, innovators like Milt Fisher over on Oregon's Nehalem River have found that steelhead *will* take a Glo-Bug fly, which imitates their favorite food—salmon eggs."

Rain had begun to leak from the van's sunroof and was tapping out a depressing dirge on the back of my seat.

"So, if we use attractor patterns do we fish flies that look like a girl steelhead?"

Guido was not amused. It wasn't that funny, anyway. The weather had turned our respective senses of humor into a pair of wet socks. I would have killed for my lost cup of hot tea.

"No," my fishing coach answered in a cold-bathwater voice. "We're going with the food-item flies, like little weighted streamers that bounce and swing along the bottom."

"Like we did when we were in Mongolia?" I asked hopefully.

"Sort of. Only we'll use pink bodies to imitate a shrimp because these fish are fresh from the ocean and that's what they've been eating. Also orange Glo-Bugs."

"But I thought they weren't eating?"

"They're not, really. But a shrimp or a salmon egg might attract them enough to take a bite."

"So are they attractor patterns, too?"

"No, I told you, they're food items."

"But you just said they might attract them."

"Because they'll want to *eat* them. Classic attractor patterns just get their attention."

"Well, if we're just trying to get their attention, why don't we try something that looks like . . . like . . . ," a sun-roof rain drop smacked me on the nose, "like that Alaska senator who hates nature."

"Ted Stevens?"

"Yeah. We could glue a Glo-Bug on its nose and call it a Bozo."

~~~~~

A placenta of rivers nourishes Willapa Bay: the Bear River to the south, the Naselle, the three Nemahs—south, middle, and north—the Palix, the Niawiakum, the Bone, the Willapa proper, Smith Creek, and the North River. I am not at leave to divulge the glorious sidewinder of a river we fished that day, under penalty of never receiving another casting lesson from Guido as long as I live, so you'll have to settle for a one-in-eleven chance of figuring it out for yourself.

Suffice it to say, Guido's river of choice wound westward toward the bay, half-hidden by the balustrade of understory that girds even second-growth coastal temperate rain forest. And so we wound eastward, tracing the river's trajectory into the higher country, back toward its headwaters. For the first time it occurred to me that I have been wrong all my life about the ocean: it is not the great beating heart of the West, the mountains are. Mountains and hills, by the sheer fact of their elevated existence, keep the planet's blood moving. The Northwest's webbing of streams and rivers really is its arteries and veins and capillaries, carrying highly oxygenated blood-water through the muscle and bone of the land, always and forever to the ocean, which is the . . . the . . . what?

"The ocean must be the spleen!" I blurted out.

Fortunately, when in fishing mode, Guido, like Dr. Dick, concentrates so completely on his mission that one can pretty much say any sort of nonsense in his presence and his compass needle won't jump. But the fact is, even when he's not fishing, non sequiturs don't throw him, because Guido is, above all, an artist with an authentic artist's temperament. He draws fish and flies as well as he catches and ties them, moves from point A to point B with the predictability of a pinball, and handles both time and money in such a mysteriously non-linear fashion that his more precise friends can only stand back in horrified awe.

Somehow it all works. Mostly, I think, because Guido wasn't given the middle name "Reinhardt" lightly. It means "pure heart" and that's what he's got. Which is why I felt perfectly safe venting the unedited products of my own convoluted mind while Guido negotiated the now snowy road in a falling-apart van beside a near-invisible river with a Pacific winter storm nipping at our wheels. I knew he could take it, if not run with it. Sure enough, he calmly replied: "Maybe the ocean is more like a giant stomach."

"Why a stomach?" I asked, truly bewildered.

"Because it generates so much nutrition, and it's full of food and water."

"Well, maybe it's more like a big small intestine," I countered, "that absorbs all the nutrition from all the fishy food that keeps breaking down in it."

"No, it's a like a gigantic pancreas that keeps *churning out*

insulin and *digestive enzymes* so the nutrition can be used."
Guido's words now flung themselves out of his mouth like
Shakespearean cannonballs. "Or," he continued, "maybe the
ocean is just a big *liver* that filters everything *over* and *over* and
over and now that we've overloaded it and its rivers with *pollution* from industry and logging it's getting *sick* and suffocat-
ing all the fish with silt and toxins like *dioxin* and other
estrogenics and that's why fishermen who kill and eat wild fish
are turning into *little girly men!*"

He was half-right. A young man today is half the man his
grandfather was, biologically speaking. A 1993 Danish study of
the medical records of 15,000 men revealed a 42 percent drop
in semen production between 1938 and 1990. A team of highly
insulted French researchers tried to neuter the findings of their
Danish colleagues, but wound up corroborating them. Some
Frenchmen tried to pass off these results as part of the Coriolis
Effect, to which they do have a special relationship since it was,
after all, named for the French civil engineer, Gaspard G.
Coriolis, who identified its existence by observing that zee
earth turns, zat which moves in zee northern hemisphere
deflects right, zat which moves in zee southern hemisphere deflects left . . . which explains why Parisians always stand to the
left when someone uncorks a bottle of champagne, and, if it
was a bad year, why it goes down the drain clockwise.

Nobody knows how the Coriolis Effect could possibly
cause an international bungee jump in sperm production.
Scientists, however, say it's more likely due to living in a world
increasingly saturated with "persistent toxic substances," no-
tably DDT, PCBs (polychlorinated biphenyls), and dioxin.
These chlorinated organic compounds have the nasty habit of

masquerading as natural hormones and end up raising hell with both human and animal reproductive systems. *Malheureusement,* dioxin is the guaranteed by-product of pulp mills that use chlorine, and the Environmental Protection Agency's famous National Bioaccumulation Study found that no one else has dumped more Little Girly Men–making dioxin into Northwest waterways. The 1987 study found 5.2 parts per trillion of dioxin in the tissue of fish taken near pulp mills that use chlorine. Fish taken near oil refineries came in second highest with 2.16 parts per trillion, and fish taken near pulp mills that did not use chlorine had only 1.22 parts per trillion of dioxin, which is why it's *trés* cool to buy their handsome, brown, unbleached coffee filters and paper towels. Nonetheless, the EPA considers "safe" levels of dioxin to be only .07 parts per trillion in fish tissue, so we still have a ways to go.

"And until we get there, a better argument for catch-and-release simply could not be made," my fishing coach advised. "Although it's okay to kill wild fish *if* the run is strong enough to sustain harvest . . . until then we should release them." Clearly, Guido isn't a graduate of the Yale School of Forestry and Environmental Studies for nothing. The links between civilization, old-growth forest, and wild fish are etched into his brainpan like a treasure map. The man is the Wise Use movement's worst nightmare—an environmentally educated activist who understands science *and* human behavior, and who regularly talks everybody and anybody out of thousands of dollars in order to save and restore fish habitat.

Both Guido and his like-minded brother, Willie Rahr, supported their father's idea of putting the family's Montana ranch under conservation easement so that it can never be developed. The place is so beautiful that visitors are tempted to honor it with a sign that reads "This Part of the World Saved." If Guido and his pals at Oregon Trout have anything to say about it, a similar sign will one day be planted at the mouth of each of the Northwest's healthy salmon and steelhead rivers.

It is one of fly fishing's truths that the most passionate fly fishermen are also the most passionate fish conservationists. The reason is clear enough: no fish equals no fishing, an equation so irrefutable one would think *all* anglers would devote themselves to saving fish. When Guido's not fishing, he serves as Oregon Trout's associate director of conservation.

In 1993, Oregon Trout awarded a grant to three of the region's top biologists—Willa Nehlsen, Charles Huntington, and Jon Bowers—to identify the last best wild Pacific salmon and steelhead stocks in the Lower 48. They defined "healthy stocks" as those that are native, nondeclining, and whose "abundance was at least 33% of what would be expected in the absence of human impacts." Their final tally was a heart-stopping 99.

Would that we could talk government agencies and private citizens alike into protecting these precious genetic gold mines from civilization and its ever-present pollution, reckless logging methods, impassable dams, diseases from fish farms and hatcheries and from overfishing. We did our part: given the way we fished that day, at least one good salmon-and-steelhead river was in no danger of losing even one degree of its healthy-stocks status.

~~~~~

"How are we supposed to cast in this *wind?*" I yelled. Guido didn't hear me. In fact, he didn't hear much of anything I said for the next five hours, because the winter zephyrs ran by and snatched every word as it left my mouth.

We had finally found a stretch of river he approved of. We'd driven up into the hills to find it, and it was cold up there. Guido ended up parking the van in a low snowbank, which made getting into one's waders a refrigerated event. But soon we were geared up, Glo-Bugs at the ready, and began our hike down the bank to the river.

"Now remember," Guido counseled, "with Glo-Bugs you fish your way upstream, not downstream like you do with classic steelhead wet flies."

"Why?"

"Because Glo-Bugs imitate salmon eggs, and eggs can't swim."

"I don't get it."

"Okay, look," Guido said. "About ninety percent of steel-heading is done with classic steelhead wet flies, which are at-tractor patterns. We cast them *downstream* and let them swing at the end of the line right by the steelhead, so they look like an insect or a little fish or a shrimp that knows how to swim. But a Glo-Bug needs to do a dead drift, just like a salmon egg would in the river, so we cast it upstream and let it drift down, completely drifting with the current, just like a dry fly. Got it?"

I sort of did. Sort of didn't. But I did know that the river was lovely. Narrow and curvy. A regular liquid *Sports Illustrated* swimsuit model, if you're a guy. To me it was more *The Wind in the Willows,* a mysterious, deep-cut place where the water seemed to hide rather than run. It was my first time fishing a real coastal river, my virgin outdoors introduction to the green side of the mountains. This, finally, was the landscape I originally had set out to know.

While Guido continued his finely focused cast-and-step dance upstream, I followed at a distance carrying his borrowed 8-weight Winston, awed by the beauty of the feral fabric around me. Salal and fern whipstitched the hillsides. Twenty-foot wild huckleberry bushes fanned out between alder and fir whose roots wove a subtle herringbone pattern into the banks. And the world was draped with the soft crochet of moss. Everything clung to everything. Biomass ruled earth absolutely, binding it tightly unto itself. No wonder steep-slope logging sends tsunamis of winter mud raging down Olympic Peninsula river canyons; when they pass, the leaves of the trees left behind must sound like a death rattle.

Not that they don't fall of their own accord, those monster spruce and fir and cedar. If you look closely in any old forest, downed trees are everywhere, leaning akimbo in all stages of natural decomposure. Theirs is an elegant geometry. Some seem new, the work of recent storms. Others assumed their places centuries ago, their elderly cellulose coming apart in blocks like organic Legos. Like the re-nutrifying properties of salmon bodies, these fallen giants feed the forest, serving as nurse trees that literally support all manner of new life—moss, lichen, and most important, the delicate seedlings of new trees.

But the forest in which we fished was as young as the river was ancient. The timber company that owns the watershed logs three percent of it each year; thus no tree in it is ever more than forty years old. Still, the intimate verdure of the place made me want to applaud. The river itself sounded like a nonstop standing ovation. It's a fine music, the song of a river. Full and sweet and constant. The more you listen to it, the louder it becomes. The louder it becomes, the less you can hear the endless gossip of your own mind.

In the rarefied air of this green, green place, with its vaporous light falling close and cloudlike from the tops of trees, I had a realization of my own: If the relentlessness of rivers gives our relentless mind-chatter a run for its money, could there dwell, deep in the rhythm of a river's steady heartbeat, the metronome of peace? Could the frantic energy of rivers, which had so repelled me at first, in fact represent one of life's inventive forces? And therefore offer us a rare opportunity to attune ourselves to it?

Surely, at the very least, therein dwelt the recipe for eternal biolife. Left to itself, even for a few years, a forest river begins to rework its natural magic. The one-celled creatures interact with the multi-celled ones. Water insects begin anew their aquatic circle-dance, and fish gratefully eat them for it. Birds and bear eat the fish. Seeds push up through their tracks, roots push down, rodents dine on both blade and seed, while pitch and pith alike run with the deep sap of terrestrial creativity.

Fractals, I thought. In any square inch of this, you can see the entire biological machine. But no. This is hardly a machine. Or an engine or motor or clock or any of the industrialized images we moderns like to weld onto whatever it is that turns the exquisite living systems of this planet. What I sensed standing there, thigh-deep in cold river water, was . . . an intelligence. The invisible powerful thing, Alaska author Gretchen Legler calls it. A knowingness that serves as parent, choreographer, and dance floor, at once creating the dancers,

directing the dance, and cradling it all in its unfathomably capable hands. Surely, this is the same force that breathed life
into this earthly design in the first place.

One thing you can say about fly fishing: it gets you Out
There where both nature and spirit reside in relative peace,
free of the baggage of the human mind—except for what you
drag in yourself. Reeling, as it were, from the power of it all,
my own busy little mind felt, for once, like a still lake. Images
not of my making began to take shape there: a six-point elk,
a glistening bear cub, or, and finally, the passionate leap of a
steelhead heading for home.

Leaping, in fact, is a native steelhead's signature. All Northwest steelhead stories say they jump like crazy things. But to
witness this you have to hook one, and, so far, neither Guido
nor I had come close.

No sooner did I lift Guido's 8-weight Winston to the
wind than the reality of my slack casting abilities flooded my
consciousness again, rupturing my moment of Zen bliss.
That's the way enlightenment is: one moment of ecstatic
transcendence, endless hours of attack thoughts. Frustration.
Anger. Blame. Guilt. Despair. Fear and loathing, of self and
others. You name it, winter steelheading produces it.

In my case, being a bad caster was bad enough. Being a
bad caster in a bad wind was impossible. Every time I worked
up the courage to try again, the wind laughed in my face and
my fly followed. It hooked my hair, beaned me on my forehead, bounced off my nose, did a rude little flamenco on my
Polaroids, and sideswiped each cheek. Finally it flew straight
into my mouth. And that's when I ate it.

It was a timing thing, really. I just happened to catch the

Glo-Bug in my teeth. Like a predator ripping flesh from bone, I grasped the hook shank with my free hand, bit a piece of the orange yarn off it, chewed it up, and swallowed it. I don't know why I swallowed the fly. Probably for the same reason a steelhead does. I was tired, cold, would much rather be spawning, and was therefore extremely irritable. I would have snapped at anything that came too close to my face. And in that moment I personally understood why every Northwest angler worth his salmon eggs says you *have* to drift your fly directly in front of a steelhead's face if you want a Glo-Bug's chance in hell of getting one to bite. Like my mother wearing a floral hat in an unconscious attempt to become the painting, I had become the fish.

Of course, eating my fly meant that I had to tie on another one, and like Haig-Brown's fingers in the frosted January of 1929, my own "were so cold and stiff that I could hardly turn the reel . . . ." But my salmon days had taught me that a fish on the line turns all difficult weather to summer. It's worth the effort. So I fumbled my way through a double-clinch knot that would have had Dr. Dick swearing in seven African languages, and resumed casting my wimpy forlorn cast, whipping the ancient Winston back and forth like a Slinky.

I felt terrible. I knew I looked worse. This was not the glorious image I had imagined—a privately noble vision of *moi,* standing tall in an enchanted coastal river, rain blessing my face like a baptism, wind singing through my wild-woman hair, my line sailing, my heart pounding, my mind going, going, then gone. No, I was certain that should someone at that moment flash my image back to me in a full-length mirror, I would have looked like a waterlogged sandwich wrapped in thick neoprene Saran Wrap . . . with legs.

Guido, on the other hand, looked, as always, perfect. Perfect slightly hunched posture. Perfect hammering-man casting motion, as his eyes tracked perfectly both the fore and aft halves of each perfect cast. His worn oilskin rain jacket blended perfectly into the surrounding rain forest—mine was a thigh-length street coat that dragged unbecomingly in the river. His hood rested elegantly on the curve of his duckbill Hemingway ballcap—I was hatless, so my hood flopped down over my eyes giving me a half-blind, derelict look. And the only gloves I'd brought were wool-lined, which meant they had begun to smell like dead rats. Guido, of course, was gloveless. The rain dripped rakishly off his strong hands as in a Patagonia ad. He wasn't even cold.

"How do you do it?" I asked him miserably.

"Do what?"

"Look like that in weather like this."

"Look like what?"

Being a guy, he didn't have a clue what I was talking about. That's the true test of Real Cool Guys—they're way too cool to know how cool they really are.

If there were such a thing as death-by-dorkiness, I would have died right then. So much for romantic notions: Zen flashes aside, this business of "I'm beginning to know a Northwest river" (hummed to oneself to the tune of "It's beginning to look a lot like Christmas") was for the fish—the birds have enough sense to stay out of that kind of weather. I was not in the most euphoric of spirits. "Daddy would *never* have made me fish in this weather," I thought.

It was true. As immune as he himself was to all manner

of climatic discomfort, my father went to great lengths to keep his daughters warm and dry. When we were tidepooling, he always brought along a thermos of chicken noodle soup to warm us up if California's famous fog rolled in. When we camped, the tent was ours—Daddy always slept outside on a cot beside our door, his .22 by his side in case we needed protection. Even the driving parts of our fishing trips were designed for our comfort; he would stack all three of our inflated air mattresses on the back seat of his old Cadillac, then layer our flannel-lined sleeping bags on top of that until they were level with the top of the front seat, and when we were tired or bored, Valerie and I would languish back there like potentates as our father drove us ever onward to our next outdoors adventure. Until I started fishing with Guido, I had no idea how much pain I had been spared.

"How long do we have to do this?" I hollered to him against the wind.

"Do what?" Guido hollered back.

"Suffer," I yelled.

"Suffer?" he cried. "This is heaven." Ice water ran freely from the brim of his hat. A similar stream flew sideways off his hands. "Just hang in there, Max," he called sweetly. "This is when you catch 'em. Focus on your rod tip. Watch your back-cast. One o'clock, ten o'clock. You can do it!"

Like a dead sardine on a conveyor belt, I kept moving upstream too. We hiked over boulders, fished their pocket water. We scrambled over snags and cast to the holding pools their prone presence created; then, clearly fishless, we paused for a morsel of lunch. Water ouzels zoomed by, inches from the river's surface, miniature stealth bombers sounding their whistling alarm at our invasion; I felt like doing the same when I discovered that the sandwiches Guido had thoughtfully prepared bore the distinct mark of having spent the last three hours in a nonwaterproof backpack. I sampled the resulting tomato and whole-wheat paste.

"Ooze-all," I exclaimed.

"Sorry," Guido replied.

Then we were off again, stomping upriver forever and ever in a storm that was of a similar mind. This, I knew, is what putting in your rod hours means. And, despite the scenery, I was beginning to hate it.

Chapter Six

BITE THE WAX
TADPOLE

"If you can't cast in the wind, just turn around."

So said the chef as he turned around to set a hot pillow of omelet in front of Guido. After a peerless Pacific pounding, my fishing coach had agreed to let us quit the river and repair to rooms at the mercifully civilized Shelburne Inn in the misty town of Seaview, Washington. Now we were being treated to a haute angler's breakfast cooked by our long-term fishing pal and innkeeper, David Campiche.

"Or find a turn in the river that goes the other way," Campiche offered as he set a second omelet into the space between my butte of cranberry-oatmeal pancakes and my teacup. "Who was it—Fritz Perls?—who said: 'Don't push the river.' And you don't." Slow laughter drawled out of one side of his mouth. If you didn't know better you'd think he was from the South. But David Campiche is a native son of this waterlogged coast. He was born and raised here on the heel of the Long Beach Peninsula, the eastern shore of which is the western shore of Willapa Bay, where he and his wife, Laurie Anderson, own and run the old Shelburne Inn.

It's a lonely little appendix, this twenty-eight-mile-long peninsula, a glorified sandspit, really, created by accretions spat north from the busy mouth of the Columbia River for tens of thousands of years. A century ago, the Long Beach Peninsula was the natural playground of well-to-do Port-landers who used to take a big white paddle-wheeler one hundred and ten miles up the Columbia, then board "The Train That Ran with the Tide," which moved so slowly and stopped so often that passengers could pick berries and go duck hunting along the way. Eventually they would deboard at any of a dozen stops and settle into any of two dozen inns. The lone survivor of that era is the Shelburne, and at the dimming of our long and fretful day of winter steelheading, its Victorian countenance glowed like home itself.

Never did a hot bath possess such restorative properties. Never was a down comforter such a friend. Never had I felt so grateful for a sturdy roof over my head as the January rains flogged my garret room like a liquid cat-o'-nine-tails. Never did I more fully understand what mountaineer Lou Whittaker meant when he said that after a week on Mount Rainier he stops dreaming about women and starts dreaming about salads.

It's the basics you appreciate most when you spend even one hard day in the elements. And never was a hot breakfast more applauded than the one David Campiche served Guido and me that heaven-sent indoor morning. I didn't even mind that my omelet looked like it was stuffed with duck legs.

"What are those?" I asked.

"Those are yellow-feet," Campiche instructed. "That's about all we can get in the winter here, that and spiny hedgehogs."

"Hmmm. Tastes just like a mushroom," Guido noted nonchalantly. After all, he has eaten jungle grubs in Chiapas while searching for harpy eagles, and both of us had survived the unrefrigerated "nuttin' but mutton" handiwork of our Mongolian fish-camp chef.

"They *are* mushrooms," David drawled. "Yellow-feet are a winter chanterelle. They're nice with oysters."

"I bet they're even better with steelhead," I sort of whined. I didn't mean to. But the thought of mushrooms reminded me of forests, and the thought of oysters reminded me of water, and there I was again, standing in that ice bucket of a river with the wind driving fir-needle icepicks into my face while I flailed away at a damn renegade rainbow trout that remained so elusive, I was secretly beginning to believe it was a myth.

Like Washington's Bigfoot or California's grunion, maybe steelhead really don't exist, I thought. Grunion certainly were a myth as far as I was concerned. Every summer of my childhood, I made my mother and stepfather wake me up at all hours of the night to escort me down our hill to the beach, where scores of little silver fish were supposed to ram the shore in the moonlight, wild with the will to spawn. Every summer we followed the tide tables: 11 P.M. one night, 11:26 the next, then midnight, then 1 A.M. And every time my hopes were crushed by the heavy gavel of the falling, fishless surf. No plea bargaining, it said. Case dismissed. Now go home, all of you.

Campiche's mushroom-colored eyes glittered kindly behind his glasses as he poured himself some coffee and took a seat between Guido's chair and mine.

"Steelhead," he said, patting me on the shoulder. "My brother woke me up one morning and said: 'Get up. I'm gonna get you a steelhead.' I told him to go to hell. 'I'm sleepy,' I said. He got me up. Made me cook him breakfast— it was before first light. We drove in complete blackness. It was cold, you know. And I was mad. Then he wouldn't let me fish for the longest time. We walked the river for a mile, we were on the Nemah. Finally we came to the confluence of a couple of streams. The place picks up all kinds of garbage—tree stumps, pieces of fence and barbed wire. I think the garbage holds the whole thing together.

"There was a dead tree there that looked like it had been cut down. My brother said: 'There's a steelhead right under that tree.' I told him he was full of you-know-what. He made me cast out and he said, 'That'll never do.' So I brought the line back in and I thought the second cast was quite good, but he said, 'That won't do, let out a yard of line.' I had on a tinsel blue hotshot. It's a lure, one of those lures that aggravates steelhead. Makes 'em mad by flopping on their nose."

I nodded with extreme understanding.

" 'Let out another yard,' he says, so I do and he says, 'Set it.' And I say, 'What?' And he yells, 'Set it!' So I do and— bam!—out comes this ten-pound hen. Jumped all over the place. Made all kinds of runs. Took about twenty minutes to get it on the bank, then my brother said: 'Let it go.' I said, 'What the f— are you talking about?' He said, 'It has some color in it, it's a spawner, let it go.' 'I'm not letting it go,' I told him, but he leaned down and unhooked it and off it went. That was my first steelhead," Campiche said, laughing side- ways. "I've only caught a couple of dozen or so all together."

"Did you ever cook any?" I asked.

"Oh, sure, some," David replied. "But there aren't very many anymore. My brother used to go out and limit every day. He was a very fine fisherman. But none of us fly fished. We didn't think you could until Guido came through and showed us how to roll a line across the water to avoid the brush." Ah, the ubiquitous roll cast, I thought. I still couldn't do one myself.

More guests had arrived, lured downstairs by the fra- grance of David's cooking, so he pushed back his chair and headed for the kitchen. He got about a yard away, then he turned back and shook his head at me.

"Be patient," he said. "The trick is that it's like an initi- ation. You have to learn the steelhead's ways. Once you do that, they come to you."

~~~~~

Just after breakfast the rain shifted from Irish mist to hanging puddles, which is what some people call certain high mountain fishing lakes. Same difference, except that when they're falling on your head they tend to dampen your enthusiasm to go fishing.

I was extremely pleased when Guido set up his fly-tying vise on the far end of the Shelburne's breakfast table. Campiche retreated to the catacombs of his kitchen, and I happily false-casted between the two of them.

"Try this."

The offer slipped Popeye-like out of the side of Campiche's mouth, but the loamy paste in the wooden spoon was no canned spinach. It smelled of forest floor and riverbank, with high notes of rosemary and raisin. I wanted to dab some behind my ears.

"Mushroom duxelles," Campiche declared. "Porcinis, butter, brandy, and fresh herbs from the garden."

It tasted like where nature-spirits go when they die.

"Heavenly," I declared, though the elixir's nut-butter consistency made the word sound more like the burblings of late-stage lovemaking.

"Now *this* is a steelhead slayer," Guido announced from the other room.

As my migrations between the kingdoms of victuals and vice continued, I got to thinking about the primal link between cooking and fishing. (The erotic connection is a no-brainer. Everything about the sport reeks of guy-sex. You know, *rods, flies, shooting line, Every*thing.)

In my own life, cooking and fishing have long been intimates, for they were two of my father's favored recreations, and he went about each of them with the same extreme concentration. Fishing was what he did *with* us, but cooking he did *for* us. In a relationship lacking in personal communion, the two activities amounted to a kind of unspoken nourishment. Seesawing between Guido's fly-tying station and Campiche's stove was like tracking the two aspects of my father I loved most. The result was a wonderful kind of masculine nurturing that helped relieve the brutality of the previous day, and set off a sweet reverie of the early days with Daddy.

While David moved slowly from pot to pan, I saw my father in his beachfront kitchen, and what I remember is a blur, because Daddy never took his eyes off his culinary creation and his body never stopped moving. The intense energy that ran him could be equally channeled into the rod or the skillet. Why? I wondered. Maybe because fishing and cooking are active meditations. They bid to move the body that needs motion while they center the mind that needs peace.

So complete was my father's attention that whether cooking or fishing he did not speak; thus my sister and I remained always observers, never participants in his process, and our time with him was spent in the emotional twilight zone known to any child whose father was ever able to share activities with her but not much of himself.

Of course, I thought, my father's father had been a stranger to him, because of his demeanor and the brevity of my father's time with him. He was a reserved gentleman of Scottish ancestry, a native New Zealander, marine biologist, and government administrator who had retired in Honolulu. My father's Victorian English mother was an equally re-

served, highly religious woman who had no idea how to relate to such an energetic boy. So, I mused, if a child has no
siblings, and learns close communication from neither parent,
it stands to reason that he'd have a hard time with intimacy
himself. And it made sense that his own children would experience him as a physical presence marked by emotional distance, a phantom father figure who remains unknowable.
The dull ache in the heart that results, I think never quite
goes away, and it's spooky how many daughters manage to
marry psychological photocopies of their fathers and how
miserable these copycat marriages inevitably make them.
There is no one to blame, of course, but the dumb-ox of disconnection endlessly circling its karmic post. One wonders,
though, if there is a way out.

The good news is that children do absorb what they can,
often the better parts of a parent. It surprised me to find how
deeply I'd internalized Daddy's love of the road and the natural world, his vital energy and his willingness to expend it
to get somewhere—anywhere—interesting, especially if it
was fishable. I think it's fair to say that my sister and I both
inherited our father's good-hearted sociability, which he
demonstrated in unexpected ways. For instance, our sister,
Heather, was technically our half-sister, yet she was always in-
cluded in Christmas at Daddy's, and remains to this day awed
by his profusion of gifts to her. "It's unusual," she says, "that
someone who is no official relation would care about you like
that." Like Valerie and me, Heather can't remember ever having a real conversation with our father, but his kindness often
showed in his doing if not his saying.

There are quirky things, too, in this father-to-daughter handoff. I still find my own tongue stumbling over the same words whose pronunciation evaded my father, ones, for instance, with their S's too close to their fricatives. "Snaps," for instance, or "consciousness," could make each of us sputter. And there's a distinctly British undertone to my own personal vernacular that does not compute with the bitchen California beach slang of my youth, and eventually induces a complete cultural wipeout. I've even noticed that my index finger naturally curls in and my thumb extends out on my balancing hand whenever I kick or throw a ball, or hold a fishing rod. Sitting there marveling at Guido's rapt fly-tying concentration, I found I even understood my father's willingness to cast over and over and over again with complete fascination, when I had for so long considered it lunacy.

Perhaps these traits are genetic. After all, two independent studies recently isolated for the first time a gene related to a specific personality trait. The fact that it happens to be for the "excitable, quick-tempered, novelty seeker" is not nearly as interesting as its broader implication: that nonphysical traits can be inherited. Regardless, I do know that as much as I love to cook, I am incapable of carrying on any sort of conversation while cooking, just like Daddy.

My father was a lean, muscular man, a sprinter, and when he cooked he sprinted—from spice cabinet to refrigerator to stovetop to oven, orchestrating the most unlikely combinations, usually into a dish he called "Hawaiian Chicken." Really, the concoction was an edible symbol of his own geographic polarities. Born in Honolulu, then raised in New

Zealand after the death of his father, Daddy made Hawaiian Chicken that came rife with pineapple, blueberries, tinned mandarin oranges, and other classic condiments of the British colonies: cinnamon, ginger, chutney, and mustard powder.

The emphasis on sweetness surely was the legacy of his very British mother, Emily Maxwell. A frugal world traveler, she met her husband-to-be on a Honolulu streetcar. After his untimely death she moved to Los Angeles. But her "Christian work" had a powerful pull. Soon she deposited her only child in the Hollywood orphanage that at the same time housed a young Marilyn Monroe, and took a steamer to South Africa to work as a volunteer missionary. She eventually retrieved our father from his orphan hell and, honoring a promise to her husband, spirited him away to New Zealand for a proper English education. But the call of Africa was strong, and off she'd go again, leaving her son in the care of his Auckland boarding school officials.

Having been born in Hawaii, which was then a United States protectorate, my father was eligible for the draft. At age twenty-one he quit New Zealand's Nelson College to fight in World War II and enlisted in the U.S. Air Force in California, the only part of America he knew. The Air Force sent him to officer training school in Texas, where he met my mother, then a senior at the University of Texas in Austin. Soon he shipped out to the South Pacific to serve as navigator, returned to marry my mother, and they awayed to California.

Five years later, just after the divorce, Grandmother Maxwell finally alighted in her son's small Pacific apartment, weary and infirm, to live out her last days with him—she had no one else. Despite her lifelong rootlessness, I remember her mostly in connection with great order and tradition: in my mind's eye she is seated daintily against the glossy backdrop of tile in my father's 1930s California kitchen at precisely 4 P.M., quietly taking her afternoon tea and chocolate-chip coconut cookies.

Daddy cooked for her then, and Valerie and I dined with them on weekends. When we walked in, the air in the apartment was fruited and spiced, so different from the herb-and-garlic aromas of our mother's continental cuisine. When Daddy's Hawaiian Chicken emerged from the oven, its sweetened meat was a child's delight, inevitably tinted yellow, orange, and a vivid blueberry blue—the very colors of the steelhead attractor patterns Guido was tying.

There were definite Hawaiian Chicken echoes in the mandarin-orange tones of the General Practitioner he'd just finished, a classic British Atlantic salmon fly for which Pacific steelhead have an affinity. It *was* a beauty. It had a little shell back made out of reddish brown pheasant feathers. "From the pheasant's rump," Guido informed me. There was a tail made of calf-tail dyed orange, a body of gold tinsel palmered—or wrapped—with orange hackle. And on the fly's back Guido had tied a tiny ring-necked pheasant feather with black tips.

"They look like little shrimp eyes," he said, "so when you fish this in the murky flows of high winter, it looks like a shrimp swimming backwards across the current. It is," he reminded, "a wet fly."

For some reason winter steelhead are loath to come up to the surface for a fly. "It's the one thing that's different from fishing for summer steelhead or Atlantic salmon: winter steelhead like their fly deeper, and the General Practitioner is a great steelhead wet fly."

It certainly had more nobility than the first fly I had watched Guido tie in China. It was the first fly I had watched anyone tie, and much as my father's creative abandon with Hawaiian Chicken helped secure my own love of cooking, that first fly of Guido's securely half-hitched the strange art of fly tying onto my list of Things-I'm-Not-Just-Saying-I-Want-to-Learn-to-Do.

To my modest credit I've already crossed off: "Learn to Make a Perfect Chocolate Cake" (*The Greens Cookbook,* p. 351, substitute fructose for sugar, and barley flour for cake flour), "Learn to Throw a Bullet" (thanks to Pat Moore, a childhood neighbor who went on to become a Stanford quarterback), and "Fish Outer Mongolia," which everyone thought was impossible, including the U.S. customs officers who were convinced we'd all just been salmon fishing in Alaska and were trying to pull a fast one. It was, in fact, en route to Mongolia that I witnessed Guido creating what just might be the most gonzo salmon fly ever tied by someone not under the evil influence of Dr. Cuervo. We named it "The Wax Tadpole."

The Wax Tadpole was not a tadpole. Neither was it made of wax. Guido, in fact, was trying for a reasonable facsimile of a small rodent. The one-hundred-plus-pound taimen salmon for which we would be fishing in Mongolia apparently had an inordinate fondness for mice and muskrat and the like, and since fly-tying supplies were as rare as a Rolex in Beijing, Guido had to resort to Dr. Dick's brand of Third World resourcefulness.

Guido's problem was what to use for feet in a muskrat fly. Fortunately, his answer was but a Coke can away. As it turned out, Coca-Cola had recently won the right to introduce the people who invented noodles and tea to The Real Thing, and Coke's little oval metal pulltabs did indeed resemble some sort of round footlets. So Guido used them. A few days later we learned that our innocent rodent-fly paws were part of a minor cultural scandal, as it was revealed that when the English words "Coca" and "Cola" were translated phonetically into Chinese characters, the resulting phrase happened to mean either "Female Horse Fattened with Wax" or "Bite the Wax Tadpole."

Despite the fact that one of our fellow fishermen, the eminent fisheries biologist Edward Brothers, gallantly rechristened Guido's Wax Tadpole the "Lemming Meringue Fly," when he used it in Mongolia it caught nothing. The only thing that did was the Swimming Mongolian Mouse, a specialty of our Mongolian fishing guides who made them out of some kind of Soviet rubber, with hooks for legs, then skittered them along the surface of the river in unsightly jerks. Taimen salmon ate them like bonbons.

Fishing is all about food, I thought, strolling back into David Campiche's domain. Local cranberries and oysters decorated his cutting board like rough jewels. Fishing is about indigenous food, I corrected. Catching food with food right there where it grows. Why else would Rocky Mountain fly fisherman John Gierach have made such a point of having "shot and eaten every grouse species in Colorado and tied flies with their feathers"? Talk about a sense of where you are.

For a long time I've suspected that we aren't a nation on

Prozac by accident. I think on some primitive psychic plane we're all grieving our loss of tribe and place, the twin anchors that have steadied our species from the beginning.

> *Breathes there the man with soul so dead*
> *Who never to himself hath said:*
> *"This is my own, my native land?"*

Sir Walter Scott would have been the first to agree that the variety of wild foods on wild land is thrilling. So is the bounty of a region's traditionally farmed foods. The culinary arts that have their roots in indigenous foods have deep roots indeed. The cooking of Provence is still fragrant with rosemary and thyme, besotted with wine, simmered in olive oil, and blessed with wild mushrooms and truffles. That's what grows there. That's true *goût de terroir,* which means "taste of the earth," not "terrible gout," though one can overdo anything.

"Have you ever thought that Willapa Bay is like southern France?" I asked David.

"Oh, yes," he replied, "We *call* it the American Provence. You can practically taste the whole region in our oysters."

The oysters in David's breakfasts aren't Willapa's native Olympia oysters—overharvesting finished them off a hundred and fifty years ago. But in the delicate tissues of the Japanese oyster that replaced the Olympias you can taste tidal salts and essence of shrimp, the conifer tea of the uplands, the sweet honey of the Columbia, sturgeon egg, footprint of widgeon, porcini spore, scale of salmon, and all the sea colors and mud minerals of that elegant boreal bogland.

Given the complexity of materials stuffed into Guido's fly-tying kit, selecting the right fly for the right fish at the right time is no less a synthesis. There were feathers and fur, threads and string, yarns, metallics and fluffs enough to imitate nearly any member of the western insect community.

"BUT," Guido warned, "here on the coast, the SALMON EGG is the real currency. They're like lollipops. After being in the ocean for two years, even nonfeeding spawning steelhead are SUCKERS for a single egg fly. They can't HELP themselves!" he howled. "It's a REFLEX! It's DES-TIN-Y!" he screeched, and pounded the table so hard my tea took a flying leap out of my mug.

"Meanwhile," he added in a predator's sotto voce, "all the bait-swingers are out there casting HUGE CLANKING spinners and OBNOXIOUS big rattling hotshots, so the fish perceives that it is under ATTACK and defends itself by striking back."

What happens, he explained, is that only the most aggressive and foolhardy fish of the run will take these big flashing things.

"After the hatchery fish come in, the WILD fish show up," Guido said with a Clint Eastwood squint. "And they're big. And sneaky. And smart. And silver. Most people don't even know they're there. A wild steelhead can lie in two feet of water and be INVISIBLE! Then they settle into the little pockets and crevices of the river. And that's when Milton catches his fish."

~~~~~

Milton Fischer. Goes by "Milt." If ever there were a name destined to belong to one of the most creative steelhead guides in the Northwest, Milt Fischer is it. And it was destiny that Guido called me up a month after our Willapa Bay steelheading ordeal to demand my presence at River House, Milton Fischer's modest but exclusive winter lodge built along some of the best steelhead holding water on the Oregon coast. Once again I jettisoned my plans for a comforting indoor weekend at home and set out at dawn in search of the impossible Northwest steelhead.

At 5:40 A.M., a full moon still skulked behind a gauze of downy clouds. Streetlight ballerinas lined the empty freeway, beautiful and triste in their long skirts of pink light, which my trusty Isuzu Trooper ripped asunder as we passed. Was it a sign? Was my femininity endangered by all this Guy Fishing madness? By six the sky had gone a clear ice blue, lit glacier-like and cool from behind and mirrored in the silver sheen left on the road by the rains of February. Spring was coming. I suddenly felt like buying floral underwear. "Naw," I thought. "I'm still a hopeless lyrical girl."

A mallard flying low dropped fast into an oval of pond water bracketed by twin cherry trees, startled pink. At six-thirty, big, loose raindrops landed so hard on the windshield I expected to see insect innards, but there was only the glassy morning smile of the Cowlitz River as dawn finally folded up the sky duvets and carried them away.

I had begun to love this long drive south from the island to Portland and beyond. I was grateful that it was heaven and earth that registered so deeply along the way, not the ubiqui-tous wreckage of industry nor the glowering double yellow frowns of golden arches.

By seven I was south enough to observe new green lace on the alders there, defying the silhouette of the Kalama nu-clear power plant, still terrifying even in defunctitude. There were other fishermen on the road with me. A Blazer slipped by pulling a McKenzie River driftboat named "Slide Rite." Two pickups passed with two more boats, one called "Pro-Alaskan" and accompanied by a bumper sticker that read "Work is for people who don't fish."

At seven-thirty I crossed the mighty Columbia into Oregon with "The Hallelujah Chorus" blasting from my baroque music cassette. My sentiments exactly.

~~~~~

"Ninety percent of catching a steelhead is knowing where they are," Guido pronounced.

Dutiful student that I am, I had picked up Guido in Portland and exchanged my beloved late-model four-wheel-drive Trooper for his falling-apart blue VW Fish-mo-van whose radio makes even Bruce Springsteen sound like he's underwater. As always, my coach pummeled me with yet another steelhead lecture as we inched along in the general direction of the Oregon coast. As always in that sorry country, it was raining cougars and dogfish.

"Winter steelhead are the rain forest fish," Guido began as The Boss warbled wetly in the background. "Their distribution mirrors the coastal temperate rain forest almost exactly," he said, echoing Steve Raymond's preface in his definitive treatise *Steelhead Country*: "Probably the steelhead could have come from nowhere else but this misty, dark corner of the world."

"Steelhead are very solitary," Guido went on. "They're loners. They come to the river one by one. Now, summer steelhead, they're the travelers. They go way up the

Columbia, the Rogue, the Deschutes, up the Umpqua. They're the high-desert mountain fish. They go so far inland, there's no turning back once they spawn, so they die up there. But winter steelhead are the rain forest fish. They're the Robo-Fish. They power up the coastal rivers with those big square tails, have wild sex, then turn around and go back to the ocean—sometimes in the same day!"

"Your own colleague, Cal Cole, told me only the females do that," I challenged.

A small frown swam across Guido's brow.

"Yeah, well, the guys tend to overdo it. They get kinda burned out. But," he added, brightening, "*some* steelhead live to spawn again the next year. And the next year! Some of 'em can be ten, eleven years old! And *all* steelhead absolutely *love* to eat their own eggs, which are basically the same as salmon eggs. That's one of the great mysteries: Why do they suck their own eggs? Is it erotic or are they just hungry?"

Highway soliloquies like this one, I had learned, were Guido's personal pre–fishing trip psych-up ritual designed to remind himself of what he knows about the particular species he's after and why he loves to fish it.

"Winter steelhead come in big and bright, fresh from the ocean," he was saying now. "I think they're the smartest. Every year somebody catches a twenty-pound steelhead, a smart old hen that's been back and forth to the sea two or three times. That's why they eat their own eggs."

"What's why they eat their own eggs?" I asked.

Guido never answered. What had been presented as an inscrutable mystery now had an equally inscrutable answer. Unanswered questions like that can haunt you the rest of your life. My longest-term best friend, Lauri Doyle, has lived with an unanswered question of this magnitude about earthworms for twenty years. Back then, a friend of hers was raising earthworms for compost. Lauri asked him if it was true that if an earthworm accidentally got cut in half, say by a compost shovel, it would, in effect, become two earthworms. All he said was, "Oh, Lauri, that's a dumb question"—an answer that forever intimidated her about asking the question again of anyone.

"Winter steelhead do cover a lot of ground," Guido continued. Now the radio static was so bad, Sting sounded like John Denver. "This biologist friend of mine, Bob Deibel, put radio transmitters in some steelhead and one swam ten miles in one day! Also, the males stayed in one place in the river, then switched positions with each other every few days. I think they're looking for females, like guys cruising bars."

A weather alert broke into our program: "Big waves from the storm will begin to hit the coast."

"And the steelhead are right under 'em!" Guido yodeled. "They're the SWIMMERS, man. Winter steelhead have tails like PADDLES!"

Then he let out a Northwest cowboy whoop. The raw glee of it must have pleased the weather gods because right then the sun just got up and bucked off that dripping horse-blanket of a cloud cover, and in seconds the old blue van was bathed in rainbows. The fresh light was still with us when we finally pulled into Milt Fischer's place, his glittering driveway as chrome-bright as a steelhead leading us home.

On the outside, River House appeared to be more or less your usual post–World War II wooden rambler. The interior explained the name River House, though Fish House might have been more to the point, for a finer ode to both angling and cooking would be hard to find. And housekeeping. Milt Fisher is an expert at all three. Another nurturing male—could I stand it?

In his person Milt is, shall we say, brisk. Mannerly, but abrupt. He moves through space quickly, changes directions often, and remains purposeful always. Mostly though, like Guido, he moves. And it is a downright waste of time to try to keep up with him. He just grins his wide, bearded, Muppet grin, makes a defensive-lineman cut through the air around him with one of his big, square shoulders, and vanishes. He reappears when you least expect it, always from the opposite direction, his clothes showing new signs of wear and tear just from being inhabited by a body that so thoroughly demands freedom.

Like the work-steady beat of a river, the curious effect of Milton's ubiquitous presence on his guests is peace. Stillness, even. It is clear from the outset that the man can and will take care of everything—all you have to do is sit. Or eat. Or, praise the lord, fish. And so you do.

"So, you're ready for a steelhead, eh?" he asked me, grinning.

"I'm not very good at this," I confessed. I felt ridiculous. That success-thing again. It was so hard for me to be that bad at something.

"Aw, it's easy," Milt answered, putting a hand on my shoulder, "if you know where they are." Then he was gone again.

I took a seat in Milt's spotless living room not far from the fire he had going in his fireplace. Everywhere, shelves were neatly filled with fly fishing literary classics. Everywhere, photographs of gleaming platinum fish graced the walls, winter steelhead all, ablaze with their otherworldly light. I sighed. They looked like icons from another universe, impossibly out of reach.

Even as I sat, Milton gave the perfect glass top of his coffeetable another vigorous polishing, then he dematerialized into, I believe, the kitchen, leaving me to admire the pretty bouquet of wild rhododendrons and tender fir branches he'd placed in a plum-colored vase at the table's center. The table's cherry-wood frame fairly glowed from regular buffings with good furniture oil, and its midsection doubled as a display case for all manner of fine angling hardware, Hardy Marquises and Ross Gunnisons, the latter proudly carrying the name of the famous Colorado trout river.

A nest of mango-colored snakes suddenly rose up in the far right corner of my peripheral vision. But it was just a clutter of Glo-Bug yarn on Milton's fly-tying table shuddering in a sudden draft from the front door. He had joined us again, striding across the living room bearing chopped wood that he fed into the fire, fir pitch and reel oil swirling in a fragrant masculine cloud as he passed. Then he disappeared into the kitchen again. What was he doing in there?

Just downwind from his fly-tying table, a beautiful handcrafted maple fly case stood against a wall. Its slant-glass top sheltered a holy congregation of steelhead flies, all exquisitely executed by Milt Fisher's own hand. There were General Practitioners, very orange Glo-Bugs, of course, replicating steelhead eggs, and red-orange Glo-Bugs imitating salmon eggs. There were classic Purple Perils and a selection of lovely

Winter's Hopes, which was originally tied by Bill McMillan, a La Grande, Oregon, writer and author of the famed Northwest instructional opus *Dry Line Steelhead and Other Subjects*. The Perils' blue, purple, yellow, and orange constellation was a Fauvist's delight: if Matisse had been a fly fisherman, he would have tied a mean Winter's Hope.

Milt Fischer's Fauve fave, on the other hand, was a Purple Egg-Sucking Leech, a gruesome construction with a Glo-Bug head, a purple chenille body, and purple palmered hackle.

"It's got to have a crystal-flash ass," Milton offered, noting my gaze. "If it doesn't, it won't work as an attractor pattern." A concept that rules behavior both on the Nehalem River and in Las Vegas.

But the true king of Milton's fly case was a fly so slender and fine that only a limited number of extremely skilled fly tyers would even attempt to tie one: the Ultra Scant Fly, tied on a No. 10 hook that many think is too small to hold a steelhead.

"But it will," Milt assured me. "Once a Colorado client of mine took a fourteen-pound, thirty-four-inch, chrome-bright hatchery hen on an Ultra Scant No. 10 with a three-pound tippet. It was awesome," Milt breathed. "Took eighteen minutes to land her."

"So, what's the Ultra Scant's secret?" I inquired.

"Well," Milt replied, "let's just say the Ultra Scant is highly effective . . . and Uncle Miltie really can't go into it any more than that."

"Oh, come on," I said. "What's the big deal? Why are fisherman so secretive about everything? Girlfriends are always swapping secrets—our mothers' pie crust recipes, new eye creams. Is it, like, a tradition to hog all the great fishing discoveries or something?"

Milton's grin took on lighthouse proportions.

"If I told everyone everything I know," he replied, "then all the great fishing holes would get fished out, or at least overcrowded. Worse than that, people wouldn't have to get out there and figure things out for themselves. Really, that's the best way to learn this sport—self-discovery."

"Oh, so it's OK if they *pay* you to take them out there and show them everything."

I knew I was fishing on thin ice, but I had to do it.

"It's a fine line," he confessed happily. "It's a fine line. But this lodge only sleeps four, and I have a very select clientele. And besides," he added with a shrug, "most people come here from somewhere else—they don't have the time to explore the area on their own."

But, I thought, that doesn't explain why Guido's grandfather refused to reveal his best Deschutes steelhead holes to his own grandson. "Competition," I said to myself. "This is just another version of guy-competition. I bet Milt's got special fishing holes he keeps all to himself."

"Of course," he said as if he'd read my thoughts, "there's some holding water I wouldn't show anyone, except, maybe, my wife . . . if I ever got married," he added with a wink.

Now *there* was a powerful bribe if I ever heard one. And she'd end up with one heck of a gear bonanza, too. Because the upper third of the wall upon which Uncle Miltie's divinely inspired fly case leaned held a forest of fly rods. Powells mostly, some Sages and Scotts, resting in parallel profusion on their racks. How handsome they were, displayed like that.

What a grand bit of interior design. Truly fine fly gear *should* be offered up as the art that it is. The metallic beauty of a well-tooled reel, the tapered elegance of a good rod—how perfectly they represent the precision of fly fishing done right.

~~~~~

Without warning a gust of pride swelled within me. "I'm *learning* that sport," I thought. "I'm out here *doing* it. Right now."

Nothing since that first sight of Guido's flawless casting in Mongolia had so inspired me to reach for mastery. Fortunately, I was about to have my chance because Milt was about to take us out on the river. Unfortunately, the wind had elected to pitch yet another demon-fit. Outside, the coastal temperate rain-forest rain was once again throwing itself upon the already-saturated earth. Worse, Milt, I soon learned, has a special method of fishing for winter steelhead that renders casting almost impossible for the novice, especially in a stiff wind. Such is the burden of using Milton Fischer's Super-Duper Never-Fail Steelhead Strike Indicator.

Guido had gone over the details with me in the van.

"Milton sneaks up from downstream," he'd explained, "fishing upstream like you'd fish a dry fly or a nymph. He drops in a little itty-bitty Glo-Bug no bigger than a real salmon egg tied to a light leader, with an itsy-bitsy BB split-shot weight and a white yarn strike indicator tied to the line—it looks just like a little puff of foam on the surface of the water. Then he casts that thing upstream, and the split-shot brings the Glo-Bug right down to the level of the fish, and it starts to drift downstream and the fish just SNATCHES that Glo-Bug like it was taking a MINT off an HORS

D'OEUVRES TRAY. And that little yarn strike indicator suddenly goes DOWN—bleup!—and you LIFT, and WHISH, and down underneath the current you see a BIG, SLOW FLASH and THERE is a GREAT BIG WINTER STEELHEAD with that little tiny Glo-Bug in its mouth. It's definitely a STEALTH tactic for winter steelhead." Guido's eyes glittered with predatory intention from behind his gold-rimmed glasses. He looked a little crazy.

Fishing with a strike indicator is also a *difficult* tactic, and a definite crazy-maker for fly fishing neophytes like me.

Milt, Guido, and I piled into Milt's beat-up mud-brown Trooper, a veteran fishing vehicle. It definitely had been through the Fish Wars; next to it, my Trooper would look like a lily-white prissmobile. Even my *car's* lack of experience was starting to bother me. So much for my new pride in rookie-ism. But nothing bothered me more than trying to cast Uncle Miltie's special steelhead setup.

It took us half an hour of toodling around before we found a clear piece of river.

"It looks like someone's doing some illegal logging," Milt announced. "Things should be running much cleaner."

Besides his full-time high-volume guide service, Milt is the Nehalem's official River Keeper, part of a stewardship program maintained by Oregon Trout. Thus he felt compelled to locate the source of the erosion that the heavy rain had turned into muddy runoff. When investigations failed, Milt vowed to solve the mystery later, then turned uphill and drove a curvy road at carsickness-inducing speeds to a little tributary stream.

Relieved to be relieved of his usual coaching duties,

Guido went off upstream by himself. Moments later Milt and I waded thigh-deep into a nice riffle and I began casting. Rather, I began flailing, having swiftly found out that casting a line weighted with a wet fly *and* a split-shot *and* a yarn strike indicator feels like trying to cast a giant tarantula. My poor line just cartwheeled in midair and landed with a fish-scattering plop. The wind sent the whole mess flying all over the place. There was stuff everywhere, little bits of this and that zipping every which way until I felt as though I were being assaulted by killer bees.

That thought reminded me of my all-time favorite punk rock band name: "Hornets Attack Victor Mature." And that set off both my highest-decibel hyena laugh and Milt's finely tuned hysteria radar.

"What's the matter?" he asked with real concern.

Hot tears instantly appeared.

Milt had been through this sort of thing more times, I'm sure, than he would like to recall. He knew just what to do. The simplest, most effective steadying technique in any coach's handbook: he took my hand. Then, speaking to me in tones usually reserved for animals with legs caught in a trap, he led me upstream to a small piece of very readable tail water. Using a minimum of line he began going over the basics.

"Okay," he practically cooed. "Now, remember, ten o'clock, one o'clock. Ten o'clock, one o'clock."

Standing behind me with his left hand on my shoulder, he maneuvered my right hand with his own. Oh my, the power of touch. I cast, of course, perfectly.

"That's right. That's right. Ten o'clock. One o'clock. Ten o'clock. One o'clock. That's *good*."

His voice was so soothing I didn't even want to ask him why he didn't say "one o'clock, *eleven* o'clock" like Dr. Dick always did. Slowly, Milt removed his right hand from mine. Still holding my shoulder, he said: "Now put it right up there at the edge of the fast water and just let it drift down. That's right. That's *good*. Okay, now do it again. That's right."

He didn't seem impatient. He didn't seem annoyed. Uncle Miltie just stood there at my side, a pillar of knowledge and wisdom, patience and amazingly good cheer, and it occurred to me that the source of his steadiness was somehow tied up with the river itself; that the forces that drive Milt Fisher are not powered by anxiety as with Daddy, but by intimacy and a clear sense of where, and therefore who, he is. My thoughts ran back to my father's fishing environment of choice. Maybe, I thought, Daddy was a saltwater fisherman because the unknowable plane of the ocean replicated his own emotional landscape and so it felt like home. But I could see that Milt Fisher fishes rivers, especially his river, because he knows it, and can know it, and therefore belongs to it as surely as his name says he does.

I began to regard my unsuspecting guide with a sweeping gratitude. I knew he assumed it was a product of his helping me execute a halfway decent cast, because he couldn't possibly have guessed that his existence, that his very life, had just solved one of the deepest riddles of my own, right there in the fast water of the upper North Fork of Oregon's Nehalem River: Daddy fished the ocean both because he loved it and because he couldn't know it, twin truths that made him feel comfortable there, twin truths that described perfectly my own relationship with him.

Milt continued coaching me into the dulling late light, noting improvements I myself could neither see nor feel, especially in that damnable wind. Casting in wind felt to me like skiing on ice—I would far prefer to avoid both.

But there we were, way up in the coastal hills, casting.

"Put it there," Milt directed merrily, "right at the seam, the dividing line between the fast water and the slower water—see it? Okay, now a little more upstream, so you get a longer drift. That's it. That's *good*. That was a *good* cast. See how naturally the line drifted—the Glo-Bug's drifting naturally underneath, too. Remember, it's a salmon egg riding the current—a steelhead knows exactly what that's supposed to look like. One o'clock, ten o'clock. That's it. That's *good*."

I decided right then that I would see to it that any children of mine, any nephews and nieces, would have their time on the water with Guido and Uncle Miltie.

He turned out to be a consummate chef as well. That evening, much to our astonishment, Milt set generous plates of homemade ravioli before Guido and me, filled with salmon he had caught and smoked himself, and with a special Thai curry confection of lemongrass and cilantro. There was a delicate Thai soup, too, and an elegant dessert crepe filled with blueberries and ricotta. As we all moaned out our pleasure, I couldn't help noting that the pale skin of the pasta was colored a delicate salmon orange and curry yellow, while the white flesh of the dessert crepe carried the distinct purple stain of wild blueberry. As if to underscore my earlier paternal epiphany and my alleged casting progress, Milt's food displayed the tricolor signature of both Daddy's Hawaiian Chicken and a Winter's Hope fly.

While our animated chef glided angel-like from oven to stove to table and back, he spoke of many things that seemed more important to him than the fact that neither Guido nor I had taken a glowing steelhead from his river. When I praised both his cooking and the fact that he'd gone out and gathered many of the ingredients himself, he stopped, coffeepot in hand, and said: "To go out and take your own game and fish and prepare it in the best possible way is part of understanding what goes on in nature, of knowing what's wild and what's real, and showing proper respect for the things you really cherish."

For my part, one of those things is the Powell steelhead rod that Milt put in my hand before Guido and I quit River House the next morning. It was my very first fly rod. I named it General Powell, "The General" for short. It made me feel strong. I left Milt Fischer with a new appreciation for the restlessness of rivers. Like him, their constancy is their strength and their purpose drives their constancy, and by these things you can genuinely know them.

Chapter Seven

OUR FATHER

My dog Tillie's Zen bird-chasing lesson resurfaced as soon as I returned to the island. After my miserable performance on our coastal steelheading expedition, her boundless capacity for happy pointlessness was a dog-send. When she looked at me with that pleading gaze dogs have, I didn't think "food" or "walk," I thought "Let's go practice!" According to her, the learning plateau is just a big playground, so who cares if you get stuck there. I had to admit, it was a compelling argument.

For very different reasons, General Powell was an equally demanding taskmaster. From the moment I unpacked it, my new steelhead rod stood at attention by my front door, reminding me that I was in training and ought to be out on maneuvers. Every time I left the house to run an errand or visit a friend or, God forbid, get a pedicure, the General gave me the distinct impression that I was going AWOL.

At the same time, when I passed him I was acutely aware of being, well . . . saluted. It was as if his very presence in my home elevated my personal rank in the United States Army of Anglers. There he was, a finely crafted instrument of battle, a many-medaled model of metal and technology, an officer of the highest order—he was General Powell for chrissake— yet he respectfully waited for me to take the lead. Clearly, the General demanded dignity by conferring it, an ingenious tactic that carried a seventy percent chance of making me turn on my heels, change into my regulation waders, and march right out to the nearest piece of open water. More often than not, I'd just join him in the pasture behind the house, and, with a bit of yarn tied to the end of my line, cast our bait to the wind.

In spring that two-acre rhomboid of wildness is so full of new growth, the very air there smells green. Again and again I'd step into that emerald atmosphere, take a deep breath, raise my rod like a soldier, and begin the drill. Imagining the top of my head as high noon, I'd pull back hard to ten o'clock. At least I thought it was ten o'clock. It might have been one o'clock. No one had ever told me which way the angling clock faced, so I just reckoned that "back" was counterclockwise—i.e., ten o'clock—and forward was clockwise. Once my rod tip reached ten o'clock I'd stop it midair, count off two, then punch it forward to—I hoped—one o'clock. Apparently, most novices have trouble with this clock visualization thing, because Guido, Dr. Dick, and Milt Fisher are forever saying that so-and-so takes his or her rod "too far back" or "too far forward." You never hear them say, "Hey, you're right on time."

At any rate it's easy to lose track of time during casting practice. The ever-shifting variables involved with each cast are enough to capture anyone's full attention. With only an imaginary, sideways clock face for a guide, I stood there trying to feel the mysterious physics of fly casting. With a spinner reel you cast the weight of the lure itself. "It's just like throwing a baseball," Dr. Dick had explained. But with fly casting, the fly is almost weightless, thus "the weight of the line makes the cast possible."

So the key to fly casting is forming a loop with the line and letting it unroll. And my line as it unrolled was supposed to carry my leader and my fly with it, its transferred momentum causing the leader to "turn over" and drop the fly daintily on the water. However, what the General and I were doing out there in the backyard looked more like bombing missions. Try as I might to unroll my line in a timely fashion, it continued to fall hard out of the sky and drop my faux-yarn fly on the faux water with explosive force. If we had been fishing a real river, our presentation would have sent every fish in the vicinity running for cover.

"Human joints and muscles are so flexible, it's possible for many things to go wrong," Dr. Dick had advised.

Duh.

I couldn't even get my muscles and joints coordinated enough to make one decent cast, much less a series of them.

The only thing I seemed to be able to do right was load the rod—sort of. That is, I could feel the energy my desperate flailing produced build up in the structure of my rod as it bent fore and aft. It was like the good hurt of a yoga posture that builds in the spine and holds itself there until you release it. Maybe it was just a function of my own poor form, but the shifting bend in my rod had a kind of melancholia to it, a solemn grace that felt honest in the hand.

"You are crummy," it seemed to say. "And that's OK."

In that flash of acceptance, something funny happened to my casting. The aching effort of the act began to lighten and each cast finally took on a momentum of its own. Forward and back, forward and back, the energy transference accelerated.

"Hey, I'm getting this," I announced. "I'm really getting this."

An almost giddy propulsion took over. Kind of like swing dancing. Was the General swinging me or was I swinging the General? Both, I'd say. One o'clock, ten o'clock, one o'clock, rock. We're gonna rock. Around. The clock. Tonight. The General and I were jitterbugging back there! Fueled finally by fluid drive and rhythm, the little V of yarn took off overhead, flying back and forth like a demented minibomber who had lost the other members of his formation, then finally given up and crash-landed into the bushes . . . only to rise again with our next rocking cast and repeat his aerial drama. All this greatly amused my cat, Puma-Man, who, true to his name, laid out one ambush after another for the luckless flyer, deeply interfering with both its cycle of aerodynamic karma and my own casting progress.

Irresistibly drawn to the sight of her feline brother leaping about in the grass like a trout out of water, Tillie swiftly joined the fray. Thus the General led, I followed, and as we rocked and rolled, our line flew out, the bomber bombed, Puma-Man pounced, Tillie attacked, I rushed to Puma's rescue, and soon the three of us were rolling around on the ground like the Three Stooges hog-tied in fly line. General Powell had no choice but to crawl along behind us on his belly and wait out the skirmish.

It was a strange setting for such futility rites, there beneath the old apple tree whose twisted black bones were already collared in a solid plane of rose-edged blossoms. Not the anemic papery ones of modern hybrids, but the dense heavy ones of yesteryear that held their curves like cupped hands carrying the scent of dimestore perfume. It was romantic back there in apple-blossom time, like a scene out of World War II, with the little faux bomber doing his doomed figure-eights above this abandoned farmland.

Once my dog and cat tired of these war games and retreated to their respective posts, there was no one left but the General and me, dancing away in that vernal light. My thoughts meandered the way they do when the mind goes on automatic pilot, reaching back to the postwar courtship of my parents, when they were too young to see the awful mismatch they really were.

"One danced, the other didn't," I mused, as if that should have been evidence enough. "Or, one smoked, the other didn't," I added. "And of course one fished, the other didn't," I concluded, then realized I was feeling for the first time my father's casting form replicate itself in my own body. Almost at

the same moment the phone rang, cutting through the air between the house and the pasture like the mean buzz of a B-52
bomber. It was my sister Valerie calling from Los Angeles.
Daddy was down. The doctors said it was serious this time.

Our father had been hospitalized before. Given his tarred
and feathery lungs, even a common cold could do it. But this
time, much to everyone's alarm, it was his heart, failing now
under the strain of simply trying to breathe.

I tried to pass it off as just another bomb scare. But when
I stepped into the shower after the call, a knowing arrived
full-blown in my mind: "This is it," the words said. "Go."

Our father looked surprisingly well. His skin was as brown
as ever, his cheeks pink, his hands very warm. But his eyes, huge
from emaciation, were frightened. To lighten things I told him
I'd used an upgrade coupon on the flight down and ended up
sitting in first class with Chick Corea, but Daddy didn't know
who he was. I felt a little cowed. You only get one chance to
talk with a dying parent, and if it's your first experience there's
no way on earth to prepare for it. Miscommunications mean
time wasted. What should I say? Ask? What were the important
family questions no one else could answer? Did Grandma stay
in Honolulu after she met Grandpa or did she take a steamer
home to London first? Details. Find out the big things, dammit.
Then, suddenly, I was overcome with the desire to have him tell
me a story. Our father made up wonderful stories, like the one
about the cucumber spaceship—but now, with his heart like
this, even one word was a work of terrific labor. There will be
no more stories forever. That childish thought, at age thirty-
something, made me leave the room.

OK. Forget the baby stuff. What does *he* need? What would *he* like to hear? You've already told him you love him numerous times. Everyone has. When a friend of mine was about to lose her father, long after I'd lost mine, she had the presence of mind to realize that what he needed to hear was that she knew he loved her. Would that Valerie or I had thought of that one. But I did my best. I muddled through. I held his hand and shrouded my shock when the nurse adjusted his sheets, giving me a glimpse of his shrunken legs. Nothing. There was nothing left of him. My God, where did he go?

All right. To deeper things. Life after death. What does he really believe? I wondered, realizing that I didn't know. All I knew was that when he lost mental focus our father repeated, "Jesus died to take away our sins," like a mantra. Echoes of his missionary mother. Suddenly I thought to ask: "Are you afraid?"

"No," he said feverishly.

This was a surprise. Our father had been afraid of something as long as I could remember. Maybe life scared him more than death, I thought now. It was time to bring out the big guns. In my case they were a little book—a very spiritual little book—by Ann Tremaine Linthorst called *Thus Saith the Lord, Giddyap!* But there were too many people around to read the passage I'd marked. The configurations changed by the minute: Valerie, her young son, Jesse, me, the baby Amber. Then me, my brother-in-law Scott, and Jesse. Then just Valerie and me. And the nurse. Then the doctor, and everyone else had to leave.

Except, of course, Zelna, Daddy's wife of many, many

years, a source of strength and grace to everyone she knows, especially him. I could not imagine what she'd gone through, nursing him through the hell of advanced emphysema for so long. I couldn't imagine denying her even a fraction of those last hours with him. My spiritual message would have to wait.

As these things go, it came to pass that on my last visit I found myself standing beside our father alone. No other family members, no nurses or doctor. Just Daddy and me. And so I told him that I had something I'd like to read to him. He nodded. His mind, despite that burned-out body, was perfect.

"OK," I began, feeling foolish. "Um . . . this is a quote by . . . ah . . . this physicist named David Bohm."

I sounded the way my Aunt Ruby drives, all fits and starts pushed by a tremendous need to get there. Daddy adjusted the oxygen tubing in his nostrils. Discomfort or intended preparation? Whatever. He'd always been a distracted listener and this was a one-shot deal: I had to go for it.

"So," I began, "Bohm says: 'Individual salvation actually has very little meaning, because the consciousness of mankind is one and not truly divisible.' And the author Ann Linthorst . . . um . . . well, her friend John Hargreaves says: 'What you are experiencing as persons, places and things . . . is really your communing with the one Mind appearing in a form and a language that you can understand . . . then you have translated matter back into its origin, Mind, and you are enjoying the one, spiritual universe in the highest form you can appreciate!' Then," I charged on, scarcely breathing, "Ann Linthorst herself says: 'In moments of rebirth, we become aware of what we have always been, in truth: individual aspects of the one, divine Consciousness, aware of Itself.'"

At that moment my father's huge green eyes widened with wonder and he pointed an index finger literally heavenward.

"That's it!" he cried.

"You know?" I replied, stunned.

"I didn't know *you* knew," he answered.

Thus began a conversation, however brief, that told me without a doubt that I had woefully underestimated the depth of my father's spiritual life. Somehow, Daddy had developed a remarkable understanding of spiritual transcendence. Clearly, it was his own discovery. He was, I knew, unschooled in the modern physics-and-spirit paradigms of authors such as Fritjof Capra and Gary Zukav. Somehow this man who had seemed forever haunted by his sense of a separate and vulnerable self had managed to internalize the subatomic fact that 99.9999 percent of physical reality is in fact empty space, and more important, the remaining .0001 percent is actually intelligent energy—the thing that will remain once his failing body is gone. Daddy had pulled a Charlie Parker. He was playing the inside of the tune.

"Jeck and I," he wheezed as Zelna stepped back into the room, "just had a conversation we should have had twenty years ago."

Oh, no, I told him. It only mattered that we had it at all.

In the end, that *is* all that mattered. Our father died peacefully the next night, his heartbeats slowing toward the emptiness Zen Buddhists claim contains everything, until his final breath sighed out from his body and was gone.

For the next two days I couldn't focus on anything. They

remain an unremembered event, a nothingness, a big time-out. I can't call what I was feeling grief, for I was not yet grieving. It was more like shock. Maybe it *was* shock. A shocking disconnect from fully one-half of the force field that made me. Or maybe it was my connection to our father and what *he* was feeling, a disorientation, the time-between-the-worlds. Years after his own death, my Uncle Bernie had visited me in a dream and told me about that phase. In the dream he was sitting in a chair beside my bed, ready to answer any questions. We spoke for a long time, but all I recall is what he said when I asked if we should be afraid of death. He just chuckled and shook his head and said, "No." Then he added, "Well, the first few days are a little strange."

The first few days. Those lost days were my father's first few days. And somehow I was lost, too. I had been scheduled to meet up with Guido in Portland and finally meet Lee Lane, the only woman in all my years of knowing him that Guido had irrevocably flipped over. The three of us were to go to the Deschutes for that holiest of entomological events, the salmonfly hatch, one of the most famous annual hatches in the West. It was the fishing trip of a lifetime, but I didn't have the presence of mind to pack, much less go.

Then, on the third morning after our father's passing, I awoke unnaturally early and clearheaded. It was as if a forty-eight-hour brain-cloud had lifted and was gone, leaving me energized and restless. "I guess I should just go on and go," I thought. And so I did.

Spring was still showing off then. It was twelve-thirty and the island was ravishing in the midday sun. The sky cornea had finally reabsorbed its winter milk and revealed the bluest all-seeing eye, shining like a piece of polished lapis. It felt good to drive along with nothing but beauty on my mind. As I approached my favorite white farmhouse I happened to look up. There in the springtime sky above me, as big as the sky, was my father's face.

It was a translucent image, like a hologram that somehow was both up there and near me at the same time. And while it was see-through, it was also vivid; and it was definitely my father's face. His cheeks were pink, his eyes joyful, his mouth set in the widest of grins, but his expression was not one I'd ever seen on his face before, or on *any* human face. It was unequivocably ecstatic.

I confess, my first thought was not one of awe, but, Oh God, this is like that Woody Allen movie where his dead mother keeps spying on him from the sky. But that was Woody Allen, the nihilist's nihilist, and the movie was fiction. This was real, and joyous beyond words.

It's fairly common for people to experience visions of recently departed loved ones. Usually they appear in dreams or their "spirit" is seen standing in a doorway of their former home, waving good-bye. But to witness your deceased father's face filling up the entire sky? I wasn't sure I ought to report a sighting of this magnitude to anyone.

As it turned out I had no choice. Soon after I arrived in Portland, Valerie called from L.A.

"This is the most incredible day of my life!" she breathed. "I saw Daddy in a vision."

"Wait a minute," I interrupted. "Did you see his face in the sky . . . as big as the sky?"

She literally shrieked into the phone.

At three-thirty that afternoon she too had been driving by herself when she looked up and saw exactly what I had seen in the Northwest sky three hours earlier.

"He looked like the Buddha!" she cried. "And he was up there, but I could also feel him all around me, like in *Star Wars* when the picture zooms in at you."

Soon after she saw him, she had to make a turn.

"I didn't know what to do," Valerie told me, "so I just waved and said, 'Bye, Daddy! Bye!' But after I turned, there he was again in *that* part of the sky! And his face was more vivid than anything around it."

We've talked many times since about our shared miracle, about what it was and what it meant and means. To me its meaning is clear: it was nothing other than "the one Mind appearing in a form and a language that you can understand." Daddy, I am sure, knew exactly what he was doing. He was, I believe, at the last possible moment, giving us the most important of parental gifts—freedom from the fear of death as well as personal confirmation of both the existence of and the perfect goodness of divine consciousness, just like all the great spiritual teachings teach. The vision occurred, after all, on the third day after his death, the Christian day of resurrection, the day on which the Tibetan Book of the Dead claims the soul passes from this world to the other. I witnessed it at twelve-thirty, my sister three hours later, honoring the only nickname our father ever called Valerie, me, and himself: The Three Musketeers.

Perhaps the Sufi doctrine of Pantheism says it best: "His beauty hath no veiling save light, His face no covering save revelation." I for one believe that somehow our father, who clearly art in heaven, cut some kind of divine deal to give his daughters a glimpse of the unspeakably beautiful realm of the spirit as he himself rejoined it, showing it to us in a way we could not miss, and in the language and form we could best understand, his own familiar face.

Chapter Eight

QUANTUM FISHING

Once you have seen your father's face in the sky, the waking world ignites with possibilities, even on Interstate 5. The spring greening of the Nisqually River delta becomes a visual metaphor for the ecological renewal of Indian lands that is occurring all over America right now; and the crepuscular cloud suspended above that estuary replicates eerily the distinctive profile of Nisqually tribal leader Billy Frank, Jr., silver ponytail and all. You find yourself suddenly flanked on each side by two white Isuzu Troopers identical to your own, one corbeled with fly rods and filled with grinning fly fishermen, the other sporting a bumper sticker that reads "Honk If You Love Cheeses." The fishermen honk at you, you honk back, and the cheese lover thinks everyone loves cheeses and honks at both of you, creating a bona fide moment of road-trip transcendence; for miles afterward the very whirring of your tires is the music of the spheres. A raven draws a dark arc in the rarefied air above your path, and driving beneath it you see that ravens are indeed bird-shaped black holes, mobile entrances to the Other Side, just as Northwest Indian creation myths say they are.

As exalted as Post-Miracle Syndrome is—certainly it's the only PMS you'd wish on your friends—it can become annoying to see signs everywhere. I had to wonder out loud if I'd ever again enjoy the simple beauty of the natural world sans mystical overtones, when a few miles out of Portland the pink-and-white glory of a tulip tree I passed became a bouquet of brides, telling me in no uncertain terms that Guido was serious about this Lee Lane woman. Perhaps my spiritually gonzo state of mind at that time explains why, when I walked into the Portland restaurant where we had agreed to meet that night and saw Lee sitting there, I thought—I truly believed—I had laid eyes upon an angel.

I surely wasn't expecting one. To tell the truth I was expecting one of those ponylike, hyperactive, excessively tan jockettes, because all Guido had told me about Lee was that she was "a blond downhill ski racer." A *ski racer,* for chrissake—like those crazy all-muscle Winter Olympics boy-girls on TV with Day-Glo spider webs all over their spandex racing suits who look like comic-strip characters from Planet Freeze-O.

The only truth to that notion was that Lee does indeed belong to another universe altogether—a better one. Oh, I

noticed a distinct athlete's swagger to her walk when she
went to the ladies' room. And she had that deep body awareness that all physical people share. But she was calm, not
manic, and graceful as snow itself. She was also perceptive and
refined, very kind and very smart. And beautiful! Amazingly
beautiful, with skin even paler than her pale hair, wide clear
blue eyes, and a smile like daybreak in the mountains. Again,
perhaps it was my own cosmically imploded mental condition, but the very moment I saw Lee I knew who she was and
forever after thought of her as a sister. Which is a fortunate,
if a little karmically incestuous, reaction to someone who is
clearly the love of one's surrogate brother's life.

It didn't surprise me at all, then, to learn that Guido and
Lee were formally engaged and the wedding was to be in
Montana in July, the same week I was scheduled to fish the
Flathead River there. It also made perfect sense that it was
Lee who saw it first.

"My God! What *is* that?" she exclaimed, almost squish-
ing her nose against the windshield.

We had left Portland and were, by then, en route to the
Deschutes for the salmonfly hatch. Lee was driving. Guido was
snoozing in the passenger seat, and I was sitting in the far-back
of the old blue VW Fish-mo-van as it lumbered over the top
of Mount Hood the next morning. Guido managed to startle
awake and I jumped forward just in time to see a most unusual
silver-green flash hang in the light blue cabinet of sky above us.

Frankly, I'd seen enough weird things-in-the-sky recently
to last a lifetime. Nonetheless, I had no choice but to take it as
yet another sign.

"Yeah, a sign that McChord Air Force Base is trying out some new three-billion-dollar weapon when we could be spending that money on fish habitat," Guido spat, literally, sending a brown geyser of tobacco juice out his window. How he could sleep or talk with a labret of chewing tobacco, I'll never know.

But Lee and I knew that what we'd seen was bigger than that. She thought it could be a comet.

"You could see one in the daylight . . . couldn't you?" she asked.

Good question. None of us knew the answer. But we all thought The Flash hung up there an awful long time before it finally trailed down into the forest somewhere. For the next hour we kept an eye out for smoke, but saw nothing. The only residual effect was our collective sense of wonder about it and my private knowing that this would be my break-through fly fishing weekend. As luck and the fish gods would have it, it was.

~~~~

"The secret to fly fishing is adjusting the leader," Guido said, sounding like a young-old cowboy mumbling through his lipful of chaw. He adjusted his leader. Then he adjusted mine. Then a four-point buck seriously adjusted the atmosphere by leaping through the front yard where we readied our trout tackle at a picnic table.

Another morning at Dant, the ad hoc anglers' village on the banks of the beautiful Deschutes River.

At the locked gate the night before, Lee, Guido, and I had

met up with Guido's fellow fish conservationist, the honorable attorney David Moskowitz, and his honorable attorney
wife, Leslie Bottomly. They had pitched a blue tent on the
front lawn and set up a couple of beach chairs there. A row
of fly rods lay three-deep against the wall beside the front
door. Numerous pairs of waders collapsed beside them like
fainted marionettes, and wading boots were scattered about
in every direction. The place looked like an Orvis garage sale.

A dry desert wind had kicked up its heels on the heels of
the passing buck. The spring leaves of the tall elm trees rat-
tled like Scottish sabers. I regarded my beloved Maxwell
signet ring: a stag in profile rising up, and the words *Revir
esco*—Latin for "forever green" or "to flourish again." The
extraordinary ordinariness of that moment burned in my
mind like The Flash itself: we are clan, I thought, doing what
our kind has done always—gathered together outside our
dwelling in fine weather, gregarious, social, checking our
tools, our weapons and hunting garments ever at the ready,
men and women together, friends working toward the un-
questioned, unspoken common goal of sustaining our lives,
there on that aeolian riverside.

The fact that we had all come for the annual hatch of a
270-million-year-old insect species couldn't have been more
appropriate. The fact that several salmonflies had just landed on
me—and on no one else—was clear and present evidence of
my anointing. I was blessed. I was healed. The fisherman's pox
of eternal klutziness had been lifted. Tears of gratitude made
fresh tributaries down my new face, giving the salmonfly
noodling around there a spontaneous baptism in waters almost

chemically identical to those of the Paleozoic swamp that had produced it. I knew it was time to go catch my first trout.

~~~~~

"Most people *never* adjust their leader."

"How do you adjust your leader, anyway?" I asked.

"Well, you build it yourself. Most people buy these pre-made leaders—they're just one long leader that is thick on one end and gets thin on the other. There are two problems with that—the thin end always breaks, and you can't switch between dry flies and wet flies. When you're fly fishing for trout, if you start the day with a dry fly, you want to build a short, stiff butt section, then a long, thin tippet that creates a long, limp leader with lots of coils in it, so the fly can drift naturally on the surface. But often, during the course of the day, you switch between dry flies and nymphs or streamers, and nymphs and streamers need different leaders. So you need to be able to tie knots to quickly change the type of tippet you're using to adapt to different fly sizes—if you switch from a tiny dry fly like an Adams to a big stonefly, you need to switch to a heavier tippet. But then, say an hour later you find another group of fish feeding on tiny dry flies, you need to break off that heavy section and tie back on a very thin section. And with prebuilt leaders you can't do that. Plus they're unreliable."

"What's the best knot to use with leaders?"

"The blood knot," Guido said.

"Blood knot?"

"Yeah, because of the volume of blood that pours out of

your fingers after you've been tying them all day. No, really, until you learn those knots, you're stuck with having to fish one kind of fly all day. You can do that with steelhead, but not with trout. The mark of a good trout fisherman is that he can change flies to match the different hatches and to match the different pieces of water that he comes to as he works his way upstream."

Guido had been going on about this leader business so long, I almost asked him to honor his Germanic roots and go put on a pair of lederhosen. But Freida's Riffle was upon us, and, thank the fish gods, any piece of classic trout water always renders Guido speechless.

Freida's Riffle *was* excellent, but it was the salmonflies buzzing around it that ambushed *my* attention. As river insects go, salmonflies are huge. Fat and huge. The ones I saw were one- to two-inches long and heavy as a finger. In truth they're giant black stoneflies, the largest in North America, but their bodies really are salmon-colored. They reminded me of the peach-skinned Sherman cigarettes I used to pretend to smoke in high school. Their wings are exquisitely veined, like miniature pieces of Tiffany glass, and their eyes look like poppy seeds. I thought they were beautiful, and was pleased to learn that their scientific name is *Pteronarcys californica*, though an unsuspected hatch would have seriously messed up any game of beach volleyball in my bug-barren hometown.

The specimens flying around at the moment had spent the last three years underwater. Now they lumbered ashore just when the trout were spawning, usually in the evening, hauling their half-spent nymphal cases with them. But a certain amount of maneuvering releases them from their physical impediment and they are free to flit and mate and fall happily into the water, where even happier trout await them. By day birds pluck them from the air. By night bats do. All insectivores are on red alert during this most sumptuous feast of the year, and the fever is contagious.

"There are other good hatches on the Deschutes, more prolific emergences and possibly even better fishing," writes bugophile Ted Leeson in *The Habit of Rivers*. But, he says, the salmonfly hatch eclipses them all.

Thus it was an honor that salmonflies were still doing a slo-mo tango in my hair, as my curls served as a sort of flypaper dance floor. The big bugs would land, get hung up, and have to dance their ancient mechanical insect dance standing in place, which felt roughly like a set of bobby pins moonwalking on my head.

But I didn't mind. It wasn't nearly as irritating as Guido's leadership training. And besides, salmonflies were my personal totem that weekend. In fact, if it weren't for natural curly hair's natural affinity for other natural forms, my natural good luck charms would have blown clean away. It was very windy.

Even without salmonflies, Freida's Riffle is an exciting piece of water. It's a pretty little thing located below the Picnic Hole a few hundred yards upstream from Dant and just below Eagle Creek (whose gravel made Freida's Riffle). It's fast boulder water, which is complicated enough to cast to without a minor gale turning your line into a flying cobra. The wind was so bad, I finally tried casting backwards. Literally. I turned my back on the water and cast toward the hills. It worked about as well as regular casting did, but the added handicap of visual disorientation eventually made me fall backwards into the river and bruise my knee.

Guido was still adjusting his leader at that point, but Dave Moskowitz was already fishing quietly upstream. I stopped to watch. I'd stopped to watch master casters all year: Dr. Dick, Milt Fisher, Guido himself hundreds of times. But for some reason I'd missed one crucial piece of the puzzle. It was something Guido had never bothered to tell me. No one had.

I stared harder. The wind pulled at Dave and suddenly changed directions, forcing my pet salmonflies to bungee jump onto my forehead, clinging frantically to the far ends of their respective ringlets and turning my hair into dreadlocks from another planet. I gently pushed them out of my field of vision.

Yes! It was true. Dave *was* doing it. I turned to the right. Guido finally had gotten his adjusted leader into the water. He was doing it too!

I couldn't believe it. How could I have missed it after all this time? Why hadn't Guido *told* me? No *wonder* I was having such a hard time learning this crazy sport. No wonder!

The wind took a turn to the west again, allowing my salmonfly friends to crawl back on top of my head and continue their impression of a psychedelic skullcap. At least I could see better. OK, I thought: now just to make sure, let's try holding it down with my other hand.

With my left hand I grasped the butt of my rod and pressed it, splintlike, against my forearm. Then I cast.

Wham! Guido's old Winston loaded like a Winchester, and even in the wind my line shot a good twenty feet farther than I'd ever cast before.

"That's it!" I yelled, sounding eerily like my father on his deathbed.

I tried the trick again, again forcing my rod butt flat against my lower inner right arm. Then I cast. Again my line laid itself flat out in front of me: horizontal lightning! I tried it again and it worked again. And again. And again. And again.

"Oh!" I cried out like a wounded person. All this time I'd been breaking the plane of my wrist and letting the energy in my rod dribble out sideways. "What a dodo!" I hollered.

"Don't be so hard on yourself," Guido gargled behind me.

"I mean *you*!" I yelled back. "Why didn't you *tell* me not to break my wrist?"

I was absolutely bonkers with the confluence of rage and joy.

"Didn't I ever tell you that?" Guido asked, with the blinking innocence guys always conjure up in times of undeniable guilt.

"That was a good cast," Dave declared, having sloshed over to join our summit meeting. "A damn good cast."

"Let me check your leader," Guido offered. Change the subject, change the leader—anything to get off the hot seat.

"Leave my @!!&!(#*#!!! leader alone!" Rage shrieked. Then Joy took over. "I can cast! I can cast!" it added in a tone usually used by blind people when the bandages are removed after successful surgery.

Among the enlightened, fly fishing is a sport based on respect: respect for the river, respect for the fish, respect for
master anglers who can cast eighty feet. And respect is con-
ferred by making a ceremonial offering of the best fishing
water, which is precisely what Guido offered.

"Take Dave's water," he said with a knightly sweep of his
hand.

"Yeah," Dave agreed chivalrously, "go up there and fish
where I was. It's pretty fishy."

Guido had called certain tracts of water "fishy" from the
beginning, but I never had a clue about what the term meant.
It seemed to carry near-psychic implications that I reckoned
had something to do with an accomplished angler's height-
ened perception—or really expensive polarized glasses.

Whatever. I took their advice and hiked upstream.

But standing there in that particular part of Freida's
Riffle, I finally knew exactly what "fishiness" meant, though
I couldn't articulate it at the time. The water just looked . . .
well, like fish were there. Actually, it wasn't the way the water
looked; visual clues such as boulders, proper velocity, or rif-
fles are unrelated to fishiness. It has to do with the way a
piece of water feels. And it felt like there were fish there. In
short, it felt fishy. Fish-friendly. Offishially fishmonized, eff-
ishiently fishified, refishingly fishophilic. And I don't mean it
felt fishy to the touch, I mean there was a sense of fishiness
about the place. And I felt it.

But *how* did I feel it? By what mechanism—or grace of
the angling gods—does one "sense" fishiness? Doing so takes
you beyond the usual realm of perception, past visible clues,
general knowledge, and logic. Because you can stand in a per-

fectly respectable piece of trout water studded with a com-
mendable assortment of big rocks, threaded with good current, laced at the edges with snag-induced hiding places, and
despite all these overt signs of fishiness, the place may not feel
fishy at all. And believe me, if it doesn't, it isn't. Or, in the
ringing words of political theorist Arnold Brecht, "In logic
there is, as some have expressed it, an 'unbridgeable gulf' between Is and Ought."

The intellectual snafu of this unbridgeable gulf plagued
me no end. And that made me think of the master of the unfathomable, Richard P. Feynman.

According to this late great Cal Tech physics professor
and Nobel Prize winner, the reassuring orderliness of classi-
cal physics fell apart once we started peering into the weird
inner world of matter. Basically, said Feynman, "One had to
lose one's common sense in order to perceive what was hap-
pening at the atomic level." Sounded like fly fishing to me.

Victorian physicists had to make peace with some very disturbing facts: light no longer traveled in a straight line (neither
does Guido's cast when I'm standing there asking him questions); light particles—photons—actually moved both faster
and slower than the preordained speed of light (so do certain
trout); without any warning at all photons could suddenly dis-
integrate (just like an ill-tied fly); and electrons themselves
really could travel backwards in time (just like the learning
curves of certain fly fishing students). Feynman was right. We
do have to lose our common sense "in order to appreciate what
Nature is really doing underneath nearly all the phenomena we
see in the world." And we have to lose it to learn to fly fish. But
that still didn't explain the phenomenon of fishiness.

At the beginning of this century, Einstein theorized that light itself comes in particle-like parcels—photons. It was his photon theory, not his theories of relativity, that won him the Nobel Prize. I turned again to Feynman—at least he told jokes—and his famous UCLA lectures, published in a book called *QED: The Strange Theory of Light and Matter.*

"I'm only going to tell you about photons—particles of light—and electrons," he writes. "Will you understand what I'm going to tell you? No, you're not going to be able to understand it . . . . That is because I don't understand it. Nobody does."

I felt better already.

In 1929 a new quantum-friendly theory was developed to explain the interaction of light and matter, which, Feynman confesses, "is called by the horrible name 'quantum electrodynamics,'" or QED for short.

In 1948 Feynman and two other physicists helped figure out how to calculate things in QED ("We got prizes for that"). According to him, QED "describes all the phenomena of the physical world except the gravitational effect and radioactive phenomena." Short of fishing in outer space or near Three Mile Island, I had no choice but to believe that QED and QED alone could explain this maddening mystery of fishiness. In fact, I have reason to believe that Feynman himself alluded to it in his "Loose Ends" lecture when he said: "So it was known for a long time that something fishy is going on."

It's interesting to note that Feynman et al. made their historic QED calculations by fiddling around with the way light reflects from glass or water. Any way you measure it, ninety-six out of every hundred photons make it through one layer of glass or through water to a given point (or fish), but four out of every hundred protons are reflected back.

"You will have to brace yourselves for this," Feynman warns, in explaining how to calculate the probability that light will be reflected, "not because it is difficult to understand, but because it is absolutely ridiculous: All we do is draw little arrows on a piece of paper—that's all!"

In order to calculate the probability that a photon passing through glass or water will arrive at a specific point (or fish), physicists make a little arrow on paper for each possible way the photon could go. Then they add up all the arrows and draw a final arrow, the square of which represents the probability of the photon reaching the point/fish.

I found this very disturbing. It meant that an angler's brain had to instantaneously register all the possible trout hangouts in a given piece of water, assign each one a little mental arrow, then add them all up to calculate the probability of fishiness in that area of the river. But anyone who's ever seen a fly fisherman read the water can guess that it's a far more intuitive process. And anyone who's actually read the water herself *knows* it is, especially if she was standing in the poetry line when they were handing out math brain cells.

I was beginning to feel as frustrated with quantum physics as Einstein was. Amazingly enough, even though he was partly responsible for developing it, Einstein never accepted quantum theory. In *The Dancing Wu Li Masters,* in a chapter called "Einstein Doesn't Like It," Gary Zukav writes that "for the first time scientists . . . were forced by their own findings to acknowledge that a complete understanding of reality lies beyond the capabilities of rational thought. It was this that Einstein could not accept." I had to confess it was comforting to know that Einstein wouldn't have liked the mystery of fishiness any more than I did. It just doesn't make sense.

Einstein also didn't like the idea that something in one place (like one of the particles in a two-particle experiment) could be connected to something from which it's separated (like the other particle in a two-particle experiment, which has been separated from the first particle). All phenomena are local in nature, Einstein insisted. This, I think, might explain Einstein's curious reaction to something my own mother told him one autumn evening in 1939.

She was fifteen years old at the time, a high school student living at home in Port Arthur, Texas. That summer she made friends with a girl at camp who invited her to her family's home in South Carolina for a week. As it turned out, the girl was quite well-to-do. Her father, a Robert Bruce, had been president of the American Medical Association and was a longtime friend of Einstein, who happened to be staying with the family the same week as my mother's visit.

"The first night at dinner I was introduced to him," my mother recalls, "but I had no idea who he was. He was seated across the table from me. It was a large table and the entire family was there: my friend—I think her name was Margaret—her sister and brother, their parents, Einstein, and myself. At one point he looked over at me and said, 'Are you studying science in school?' His accent was so thick, I could hardly understand what he said. I said, 'No, I'm going to be a journalist.' 'Well,' he said, 'have you ever heard of the theory of relativity?' And I said, 'No, sir.' 'And what do you think a theory of relativity might mean?' I sat there and stared at my shrimp cocktail and suddenly I got an idea, and I said, 'I think I might know what it is.' Everyone was staring at me in complete silence. 'I can prove that you and I are touching,' I said. 'How can you prove that?' Einstein asked. And I said, 'I'm sitting here, I'm touching the air, the air is touching the tablecloth, the tablecloth is touching the air that's touching you. So, I'm touching you.'"

My mother did not become a journalist. She became a clinical psychologist known for her pioneering work in human intelligence and education, with special emphasis on relational thinking. Einstein never did respond to her impromptu theory of relativity. In fact, he never said another word to her for the remainder of her visit. One interpretation of his strange reaction is that he found her idea too ditsy to waste his time on. But this is out of character; Einstein was known for his interest in tutoring young minds, which probably inspired him to ask my mother questions in the first place. So I suspect something else.

Of course my mother's idea didn't have anything to do with Einstein's special or general theories of relativity. Those involve complicated things such as the constancy of the speed of light, space-time, mass, velocity and moving clocks, though time *did* brutally slow down after my mother answered Einstein's question. But symbolically, her innocent reply just may have hit a very sensitive nerve, because in principle hers was a truly quantum idea. And just four years earlier, in 1935, Einstein's famous attempt to discredit quantum mechanics as a "complete" theory kind of blew up in his face. The Einstein-Podolsky-Rosen (EPR) thought experiment, as it is called, "inadvertently illustrated an unexplainable connectedness between particles in two different places," writes Zukav. "The particle in area A seems to know instantaneously the spin status of the particle in area B." This presupposed an almost telepathic, faster-than-the-speed-of-light, nonlocalized kind of communication. And Einstein didn't like it.

But I did!

Because it meant that objects that have been previously "correlated," such as a fisherman and fish (or dinner guests), can indeed experience an instantaneous communion: if fish are there, regardless of how much space and water separate them, real fishermen know it.

"When 'separate parts' interact with each other," Zukav offers, "they (their wave functions) become correlated . . . . Unless this correlation is disrupted by other external forces [as in, a fisherman stops fishing to take up golf] the wave functions representing these 'separate parts' remain correlated forever . . . . [And], if the Big Bang theory is correct, the entire universe is initially correlated."

"Thus," sums up David Bohm, professor of physics at the University of London, "one is led to a new notion of unbroken wholeness. Parts are seen to be in immediate connection, in which their dynamical relationships depend, in an irreducible way, on the state of the whole system." Which was exactly what I had tried to tell my father and what my father had, upon his death, proven to me to be true.

The word that comes to mind is intimacy. The closeness that comes from closeness, an immutable and intrinsic partnership with being, so wonderfully expressed by the lifelong dance between bewitched fly fisherman and fish.

Writes Zukav: "According to quantum mechanics there is no such thing as objectivity. We cannot eliminate ourselves from the picture. We are a part of nature, and when we study nature there is no way around the fact that nature is studying itself."

(Does the fish recognize the fisherman?)

John Wheeler, a well-known physicist at Princeton, writes: "May the universe in some strange sense be 'brought into being' by the participation of those who participate?"

Perhaps, then, the solution to my fishiness problem was stunningly simple. Perhaps neither fish nor fishiness exist unless and until we anglers think they do. Perhaps it is simply a matter of aligning one's mind with the probability of fishiness by the repeated and intimate act of fishing. And perhaps that alone, more than knowledge or skill, creates the fish/fisherman correlation, which explains why time after time the great fly fishermen catch far more fish than anyone else. Perhaps they simply expect to, and by virtue of their presence on rivers and the constancy of their intimacy with fishing, they literally bring fish and fishiness into being.

~~~~~

Quantum physics explained why I knew fish were there and how I knew why I knew. I aimed at the little seam between the fast water and the slower water about three feet downstream from the biggest boulder in Dave's stretch of the Deschutes. I cast. A fish rose. I missed it.

I locked my wrist again, cast to the fishy spot, another fish rose. I missed it, too.

I was, I should mention, fishing one of Guido's custom-tied salmonflies. They're a classic attractor pattern, called The Stimulator really, with an elk-hair tail and wing, orange yarn body, and a palmered brown hackle (meaning chicken-feather wrapped sideways around the hook shank, so it splays out like Einstein's hair). But Guido ties them sparsely, "so they ride low in water like a real salmonfly." He contends that most store-bought ones are so bushy they don't look like salmonflies anymore, which explains why he had grabbed one out of my fly box that morning and viciously attacked it with a pair of scissors. Lee thought he'd just had too much coffee, but I suspected the Lucky Charms: any "food" that looks like dyed Styrofoam has to wreak havoc with the blood-brain barrier.

"Why don't you just *try* some All One powder," I had urged. "It's got every vitamin and mineral and amino acid you need in it."

"That's that stuff you tried to get me to take in Mongolia, isn't it?" Guido had answered.

"That's the reason I *survived* Mongolia."

"Naw, I just want my Lucky Charms."

"All One would *protect* you from your Lucky Charms! And from smoking. That's why my father . . . "

I had been about to go into our old "If you'd seen what it did to my father you'd quit smoking" routine, but something had stopped me. A pressure. In my own chest. It felt hard, and heavy, like something stuck.

Strange, I thought, remembering it on the water now. The physical action of casting hadn't seemed to trigger it. The trigger seemed to be a thought, or series of thoughts. It had something to do with memory. Maybe the pressure wasn't a physical thing at all?

Casting Guido's Stimulator fly stimulated all sorts of responses in the animal kingdom. It looked so much like a real flying salmonfly that I began to attract swallows. I expected bats any minute. All of which was a little unnerving since my personal salmonfly-à-la-tête menagerie had grown to more than half a dozen. And as soon as Guido's fly landed, another rainbow trout came hurling at it from six feet below, swimming so fast it couldn't control its speed and burst out of the river with *Alien* shock value.

I cast again. And in that hanging moment between release and contact, the atmosphere began to fizz. "That's it," I said out loud. "That's the cast."

The clash of the photons claimed the very air, and I saw the green surface of the river give way. The moment seemed to stretch and smooth, to slow and accelerate all at once. I heard Stevie Ray Vaughan rave on, playing a tune fast and hard like a syncopated, correlated articulation of eros and care. Then Van Morrison raved on, "Down through the ages, down through the industrial revolution, and empiricism, and atomic and nuclear age." And Taj Mahal's Voice of Freedom sat in. "If they ask you, was I runnin', tell 'em I was flyin'." Peter Falk flew by on *Wings of Desire*, an angel in six German hats: "When the child was a child it wanted the stream to be a river, the river a torrent. When the child was a child it didn't know it was a child. Everything was full of life and all life was one." Testes do their slow gyrations in your hand—the true music of the spheres. The wheat germ and raw zucchini fragrance of semen. The gardenia scent of a healthy woman. Together they make love. And salt. Breakfast. Beaded Mexican snakes. Ornamental shrubbery. Trilobites.

The old rhythm of that long-gone river traveled from muscle to bone. A million gallons of heavy molecules pushing until there was neither position nor velocity, particle nor wave, no space and absolutely no time. Until there was nothingsolidleft. Nohand Norod Noline Nofly Nowater Nosky.

And the salmonflies were my hair and they weren't. *Guido* meant "guide" and it didn't. First there is a mountain, then there is no mountain, then there is. Then there is only intelligent energy shooting through empty space, the subatomic surprise, the Baha'is' Most Hidden of the Hidden, the mind of God. Nearness to it or remoteness. Peace or terror. Joy or depression. Our choice. This is the plane of *Free Willy* and free will.

My fly landed on the water. Ice ages and epochs had passed. Years had gone by. I'd forgotten everything. The nature of the neighborhood. A river and fishing. Yes, I am fishing. This is a river and I am fishing and that, by God, is a fish! My first fish! Glory hallelujah, we're back in Newtonian physics. Phishics! Fizzics! Phish on!

The playful trout took Guido's salmonfly fly for a wild ride. My reel spun crazily, spritzed my shaking hands. Another anointing. Another blessing. Restitution. Say amen, somebody. Call me skunked-no-more. It was a Deschutes native redsides, a big fat rainbow trout with an elegant constellation of black spotting on its back and comets streaking down both flanks, exactly the color of the crimson line my mother saw arcing in the air between her shrimp cocktail and Albert Einstein's more than half a century ago.

Chapter Nine

GIRLFRIENDS
IN THE FISH ZONE

"Con-GRAT-u-LAY-tions!"

The applause in Lee's voice reached me where I stood, not even halfway up the long path from the Deschutes River to Dant. News of a fish always precedes the fisherman at the end of a victorious day, and Lee was there to make sure I received my just reward.

I *had* fished hard.

Once I had caught my first serious trout, Guido's true fishing instincts had swung into action. Wasting no time reveling in the triumph of either student or teacher, he left Dave Moskowitz to his own devices and fished right behind me the rest of the day. I no longer pestered him with endless questions and confirmations; I had finally entered The Fish Zone, that sacred space where Guido himself had set up permanent residence so long ago. Finally we were partners in this most unforgiving of sports.

The Fish Zone is really just an expanded state of Fishiness Awareness. Rookie fly fishers are clueless about its existence, intermediates aspire to it, extreme anglers live there. When you're in it with someone else, neither of you says much. There is little to say. Because anyone occupying the same Fish Zone knows the same things at the same time; like correlated particles your communication is instantaneous.

But old habits die hard. So do old responsibilities—just ask your parents. Guido continued to assail me with the occasional professorial command, especially when there was anything to do with possible leader adjustments, but that day either I'd finish his sentences for him or I'd already be doing what he was about to tell me to do before he got the words out of his mouth.

If Dr. Dick had been there, we would have worked the river up one side and down the other. But he wasn't, so we couldn't fish Deschutes Club water and stuck to the west bank. That was more than enough. The trout were near-delirious with salmonfly fever. It made them reckless and fast. Armed with my new casting acuity and extra-fisheriness perception, I was a lethal angler. I hooked many, lost few, released all unharmed. When I hooked one big rainbow near the Dant boat dock, the fish took off downriver so hard, Guido had to leap up onto the dock so I could hand my rod off to him, scramble ashore, and sprint around to the other side, where I almost belly-flopped back into the water to take over my rod again. Relay fishing.

But, as pilots who fly jets describe it, in the long stretches between moments of panic, things are measured and calm. There is a wedge of silence in The Fish Zone. Its apex is the midriver point equidistant *from* each fisherman. Its sides flare out from that point *to* each fisherman. Its back edge is the riverbank running *between* the fishermen. And in that cuneate kingdom a wonderful camaraderie grows. Intimate conversation is not its heart—being there is. Being there with one's focus on something other than oneself. For those capable of surrendering to it, The Fish Zone offers a perfectly egoless adventure that can easily slide into a kind of exaltation. This, I believe, is why men who fish well together can fish standing a hundred yards apart, say practically nothing to each other all day, and emerge at dusk feeling monumentally bonded. We women have trouble understanding wordless intimacy because few of us ever experience it. And fishing, until fairly recently, has pretty much been a guy-thing.

It occurred to me standing there in The Fish Zone that women might benefit greatly from an all-girlfriend fishing trip. Women's exemplary wave-function is highly interpersonal (interparticle), and we tend to define ourselves by our emotional links (wave-functions) with other people (particles). In very real terms this keeps us trapped in particle-consciousness. Beautiful and strong is the safety net women's endless crosstalk weaves, but in the heart of The Fish Zone the life I call my own vanished completely. I needed no emotional support. There was nothing to analyze, nothing to consider, nothing to catalogue, process, decide, work through, or act out. No longer did I linger in the intricate webbing between lives; I had become simply a thread in the web. I was the wave and the wave was me and the omniactive tufting of the river was like the eternal dance of Shiva, creating, destroying, and creating again forever. All self-consciousness drowned in that watery choreography, and the peace that comes from that sort of mercy-killing is holy indeed.

It's no small feat to achieve a genuine state of grace in an era marked by restlessness. That it is the gift of the manic motion of rivers struck me as the sweetest irony. I could scarcely recall my early allergy to their endless rollicking, my discomfort at their nonstop force that would sooner run you down than offer you any solace. As for the comfort of oceans, it now seemed anonymous and sad, like having sex with someone you don't know or love.

Certainly you can love an ocean—many of us do—but I believe you can't know one, especially once the shore is out of sight. Oceans are too big, too out of human scale, too changeable, too bereft of landmarks, and too uncorrelated to our own element, the earth. What I once mistook for constancy—the predictability of ocean tides—I now saw mattered mostly in relationship to the shore; given their surface area, oceans relate very little to land, and therefore very little to us two-legged creatures who live here. Oceans present two choices to the angler: surf fishing from a beach or jetty to stay clear of endless wave assaults, or boat fishing atop an unknowable blue plane that reaches forever toward an unseeable end. Either way, the work is hardly intimate.

Rivers, on the other hand (or foot), are defined by the terrain through which they travel. Anglers always have a point of reference on a river, a place to stand and take stock, a handy place from which to enter and exit this mysterious element of fishes. The land holds the river in a complete arc. In river time, water and earth are equal partners. This, I think, gives river fishing great balance and offers anglers great security. You can take chances, challenge your body, push farther and deeper into the current, and if you overextend and go swimming you know the shore is always close by, waiting for you like a mother.

River fishing allows anglers immersion in water without their having to leave solid ground. The act of being held by water has long registered on the human psyche as a religious experience. Fishing writer Lorian Hemingway puts it beautifully: "I remembered being baptized in the street waist-deep in water, by this ravine in flood season, when the waters swelled over the lip and bore snakes and turtles and frogs on its rampage."

Good things come to she who wades.

There was no doubt about it: I had fallen in love with moving water. How? When? I don't know. Where does the hand become a thumb, the land a peninsula? In *Mastery*, George Leonard says it doesn't matter: "When you reach the top of the mountain, keep on climbing." The truth is, if you stick with it long enough, the hypnotic properties of casting, and trout streams, become their own reward.

I had to admit that the transcendent quality of life in The Fish Zone might put—dare I say it?—*guys-who-fly-fish* a little closer to God than girlfriends are. Theoretically, this would put *girlfriends-who-fly-fish* just about square in God's lap. It certainly was worth a try.

I could think of half a dozen women friends who would probably want to go on an all-women fishing trip. But where should we go? This had to be a *classic* fishing trip, a real destination, somewhere the girls wouldn't forget . . . and most likely somewhere that wouldn't forget the girls. Then I got it.

"Montana!" I hollered.

How should we get there? Drive? No, too slow—no woman I know has that kind of time. Fly? Too expensive. The train! And we can all get . . .

"*Sleeper cars!*" I yelled.

"So, you're taking the train to the wedding?" asked Guido, my non sequitur–friendly coach. He had come over to check my leader.

"I just checked it," I said. "What wedding?"

"*My* wedding," he said. "July 15. Great Falls, Montana."

I couldn't believe it. The first all-girl fishing trip I plan has a head-on collision with my fishing coach's wedding. It was to be the first of many obstacles, all of them somehow related to the men in my girlfriends' lives.

"There's no way you could go with us in July, is there?" I asked Lee back at the house that evening.

"Not with the wedding," she replied a little wistfully. "But it sounds like *so* much fun. Fishing with women would be . . . different," she said. "I always think of fishing as my way of being with Guido. It's the only quiet time in his life."

"It was the only peace in my father's life, too," I said. Sorrow pressed lightly against my heart. It still felt foreign. The heavenly miracle of my father's face in the sky had veiled death's earthbound gravity for me. Or subsumed it. Transformed it. Negated it. Something. Just remembering it sent sorrow scuttling back into its hiding place. When my thoughts rested upon him, they had flooded not with his habitual earthly angst but with the superhuman joy of his final good-bye.

"That look," I thought, recalling his face in the sky. There was no way to explain it; we just don't see it down here. Down here we swim in what David Bohm calls "the river of sorrow of mankind." Before seeing his face in the sky, my most powerful visual memory of my father had been of him standing distant and alone on his private fishing jetty. What a perfect symbol of his alienation, I thought. Now *that* was part of Bohm's sorrowful stream. *That* deserved grieving over, not the exalted liberation of his death. And isn't it odd, I thought, that the isolation of fishing gave my father peace while fishing gives me peace through a sense of absolute connection.

The deep light of early evening fell soft and violet on Lee's eyes. The quietude of the hour had turned her philosophical.

"I do enjoy fishing," she mused, "but I'm clearly not obsessed. For men, fishing becomes an obsession. It's something to lose themselves in, and I don't think men really lose themselves in many things."

"Maybe football," I offered.

"Yeah," she agreed. "But football is a kind of projection. Fishing or golf is mystical. Fishing only with women . . . hmmm."

A small question swam across her brow as she tried to imagine it.

"I wonder if other women would love fishing for the same reasons I do. Just to be close to the earth, to moving water and living things. How many things can you do in the outdoors where you actually interact with living wild things? When you hunt, you don't get to touch the live deer, you don't get to touch the birds. But you get to hold a fish in your hand. And they're such individuals! I've never caught a fish that was like the one before it. And I've yet to kill a fish.

"I could kill a hatchery fish, I think, though," she added.

"Me, too," I confessed.

Guido had taught us well.

~~~~~

Every one of my girlfriends wanted to go on the All-Women Montana Fishing Trip. Many of their close girlfriends wanted to go, too—women I'd never even met. And none of them fly fished. We had definitely hit a latent adventuress nerve. Soon my roster was spiraling out of control: a dozen women had committed. It was going to be the fishing trip of the century.

But a month later my fisherwomen were falling like salmon-flies. Their reasons for dropping out began to sound like variations on "The Modern Woman's Theme Song": Their husbands had scheduled a business/golf/fishing! (in one case) trip and they couldn't afford or wouldn't be comfortable hiring a sitter for that many days (five). Or they'd already used their vacation time on family trips and their bosses refused to give them more time off. Several had received wedding invitations they felt they couldn't turn down. Some discovered that that was the only week their mothers-in-law could visit all summer. A few had to take their family vacations then because their husbands had a slow time coming up at work. When it got right down to it, most of the women just couldn't figure out how to clear that many days in the quagmire of their normal lives.

It was obvious that working wives and mothers either can't or don't know how to take private travel time for themselves, mostly because they take their responsibilities to their husbands and children very seriously. It was also clear that, for women, personal adventure carries a serious and glittering allure akin to forbidden fruit: they really want it, but they figure they'd better not take it. The question that kept coming back to me was this: How is it that guys manage to take at least one all-male pleasure trip every year without any sense of irresponsibility whatsoever?

"Because we always cover for them at home," Rande replied flatly.

In the end, she was the one girlfriend who managed to go fishing in Montana with me. Fortunately, Rande has been my soul-sister and roadtrip buddy for more than twenty years. From luxuriating in Paris to roughing it in Alaska, we've never had a bad time together. Montana would be a breeze, I thought. As it turned out, it was more like a typhoon.

~~~~~

The Amtrak *Empire Builder* pulled out of Seattle at 5 P.M. on a Friday. The world outside had Tourette's syndrome. Downtown traffic moved in anguished stutters from green light to red. Freeway entrances convulsed with more moving metal than the city was built to handle. But in our sleeper car all was calm.

All was small, too. There were two nicely upholstered seats facing each other that turned into the lower bunk when pushed together, like drunks sliding under the table. Then the upper bunk folded down from above. Towels and coat hangers were stashed in such unlikely compartments, we didn't find some of them until morning. Cool air arrived via our own set of miniature vents. Music and announcements reached us through tiny, powerful speakers. A heavy, draped metal door resoundingly shut out the rest of the train, and the entire outside wall was a picture window on the frantic world. It was hard not to feel smug.

"You know what's so neat about this train," Rande concluded. "It's not I-5."

Actually it was lucky for Seattle that Rande and I had elected not to drive. A multitalented artist and high school art teacher, Rande is as directionally dyslexic as I am, which tends to cause confusion behind the wheel. I must say, though, that our shared afflictions have a curious way of canceling each other out: If Rande drives and I navigate and I say "turn left" but mean "turn right," she turns right anyway because that's what her brain hears . . . and we always get there. Obviously, my teaching her to fly fish was going to be an experience.

Besides switched brains, Rande and I have another quirky trait in common: we can't drink. Two sips of anything alcoholic and our delicate brain chemistry goes on Goofy cycle. Then we fall asleep. Not exactly party-animal material. But this *was* a fishing trip and we *weren't* driving, so when a Lou Rawls voice announced through our speaker that they were serving Tequila Sunrises in the snack bar, we fell in line behind a dozen other hopeful passengers.

"I thought Lou Rawls was dead," Rande said.

"Apparently not," I replied. "Maybe this is his day job."

"At-TEN-tion. May ah have your at-TEN-tion, ladies and gentlemen," the dark-chocolate voice drawled again. "We are now serving Tequila Sunrises . . . in the snack bar, baby. Thank you. Thank you very much."

"God, that voice makes you want to take all your clothes off," I whispered to Rande.

"I bet he can sing, too," she whispered back.

I gave Rande my best Tina Turner pose and then, in my lowest possible Motown voice, sang: "Hold me! Squeeze me! Please me! Bay-bee! I got-to-got-to-got-to-got-to . . . have the number of yo' sleeper car, baby!" Of course I really sounded more like Good Witch of the North–meets–Vanna White, but girlfriends overlook those kinds of details.

~~~~~

"Why is this thing the color of Ty-D-Bol . . . baby?" I asked Rande, peering into the goblet of radioactive blue liquid.

"Oooo, this drink is *strong* . . . baby," Rande answered.

The Puerto Rican bartender raised an eyebrow.

"Hey, hwee don' mess aroun' . . . babee," he said back, giving Rande the eye.

"Neither do we!" I chirped for some reason.

"No . . . We . . . Don't," Rande sputtered. As shy as we really are, exotic drinks and flirting are at best false advertising. It was high time to hightail it back to our sleeper car. By the time we got there both of us had reached our two-sip limit, so it was bedtime again anyway.

"How do you get this thing off the ceiling?" Rande asked. Knowing I'm somewhat claustrophobic, she had graciously offered to take the top bunk and was standing with one foot on one seat and the other foot on the other trying to liberate the thing.

"Just don't drop it on my head, OK?" I warned.

Rande is the ultimate Project Person. She's one of those rare women who can and will make anything—from a camper for her truck to a complete set of hand-thrown dishes to a perfect apple pie. She has the strongest and fastest creative energy I've ever seen, and when it shifts into high gear, you'd just better get out of the way. Especially, I reckoned, if it's fueled by Cuervo Gold.

"This train feels like my pottery wheel," Rande announced. The rocking motion of the car had her doing a weird splay-legged aerial rhumba. I prayed that it wouldn't send the two seats she was standing on clamping together like something out of *Jaws*.

"It . . . should . . . just . . . unsnap right here," she advised from somewhere deep in the upper cushions. I could no longer see her head. "I got it!" she cried finally, and the bunk came flying down so hard that it blasted her backwards, straight into the arms of the conductor, who had just stepped into the doorway.

"May ah be of service, ladies?" he offered, gently setting Rande down on the floor.

"It's Lou!" I breathed.

"Oh . . . no, thanks," Rande replied, much embarrassed. "Uh, I think we figured it out."

"Well, all right," Lou said, his voice falling over us like the aftershave of the gods. "Let me give you your linens, then. Now you ladies have a good night's sleep, you hear?"

We did, actually, once Rande got herself catapulted into the upper bunk. The last thing I remember before drifting off was Mr. Rawls announcing that *Sleepless in Seattle* would be playing in the lounge car, baby, and Rande's muted voice mumbling through the upper bunk's complicated system of cloth straps: "I feel like I'm in an insane asylum."

Chapter Ten

WHITE WINGS IN THE MORNING

I had lined up one of the most famous fishing guides in western Montana for our trip: Steve Smith. There was a message from him when we arrived at the lodge the next day: "Get settled in. I'll call you in the morning."

Settling in didn't take long because our room wasn't much bigger than our sleeper car. There was a bed on one side, a futon-daybed on the other, and a nice new bathroom took up the rest of the space. But it was a corner room and it did have two windows, one looking out on the train tracks, the other looking onto the parking lot, where a large bulldozer was loudly moving dirt around. Then the floor started shaking.

"Earthquake!" yelled Rande, who was also raised in California.

"No, it's just a train going by," I assured her.

"Peace and quiet in the country. Let's get outta here."

As travel brochures would have it, the lodge wasn't nearly as well situated as the photos had led us to believe. The Flathead River, which we'd come to fish, was nowhere to be seen. We decided to cross the tracks and head for what appeared to be a hilly forest studded with houses. Not exactly wilderness, but we soon found ourselves strolling down a pine-lined dirt road. That's when I got Bad-Bear Vibes.

I've traveled enough in Alaska to know Bad-Bear Vibes when I feel them. "OK, OK," Rande finally agreed. "Let's go back and have an early supper."

Seconds after we'd taken our seats at a window table, Rande said, "Look at that chimpanzee running across the railroad tracks!"

"*Rande!*" I cried. "That's a *bear!*"

Sure enough, a yearling black bear was loping toward the lodge from the direction we'd just walked in. He looked lost. And a little angry.

"His mama probably just kicked him out of the family so she can raise this winter's cubs," I explained.

"He looks skinny," Rande said with maternal concern. "I hope Elijah's all right," she added, meaning her teenage son.

"You'd better hope Glen's all right being home alone with him," I countered, meaning her husband.

"Oh," she said, waving her hand, "they'll probably just go out for pizza every night and have a great time."

To her credit, other than check-in phone calls, it was her last domestic thought of the trip. We had other worries, anyway. Like what to do on a Saturday night without a car in a lodge miles away from anywhere.

After dinner we wandered downstairs and found a couple of large rooms that would have been Fun Central if there had been people in them. But they were deserted. There was a full bar, Ping-Pong tables, a jukebox, and several pool tables.

As long as I've known her, Rande has been a fan of the 1940s—clothes, music, all of it. So when she found some Andrews Sisters tunes listed on the jukebox, she was thrilled.

"But it only takes half-dollars!" she wailed. "We haven't had those since the 1940s!"

We moved on to the Ping-Pong tables, but there were no paddles anywhere. Nor was there a bartender.

"Let's play a game of pool," I suggested.

Rande put a quarter in the slot, but no balls came out. At that moment a staff person walked in, lifted the pool table, and slammed it down on the floor. A few balls trickled into the tray. She sighed and walked over to the bar for more quarters, then deposited one. One more ball came out. She deposited another and the rest of the balls avalanched forth.

"I'm gonna be closing in ten minutes," she declared.

"Can we buy drinks?" we asked.

"How about some half-dollars with our change?" I asked.

The staff person gave us one half-dollar and a bunch of quarters, then vanished. I put the fifty-cent piece in the jukebox and nothing happened.

"It's unplugged," Rande noted, and plugged it in.

Still nothing happened.

We took our watered-down drinks into the morguelike pool room and racked the balls, then I broke. It was a good break. Two solids ended up in two pockets.

"I've never played this game before," Rande confessed, and proceeded to hit the cue ball into a side pocket. We never saw it again.

"OK, we can use *any* ball to hit any other ball."

She immediately sent one of her striped balls twirling madly into a corner pocket.

She shot again. The end of her cue stick stayed three inches above the table. Two more stripers went careening into the same pocket.

"Air pool!" she said, charmed.

She took another stroke and another two balls ricocheted into the far corner pockets. She hit again; the pool cue flew out of her hands and torpedoed two more balls, one leaping magically over the other, into yet another pocket.

Only the eight ball was left, and I explained to Rande that she had to "call" the pocket. She did. And with a single stunningly fast hit sent it speeding into the proper orifice as if it had been shot out of a cannon. Rande threw her hands up in surrender.

"That's it!" she said. "Game's over. No more pool games, ever. I could *never* do that again."

~~~~~~

Our microliter of alcohol led us to yet another early retirement. Passing trains filled the wilderness with the metallic screams of industry, and the night-winds of the Rockies crisscrossed our room. So did drowsy girl-talk.

"It's really different being on vacation without Glen," Rande was saying.

"Yeah, no sex," I replied.

"No," she laughed. "It's . . . peaceful. Traveling with you is like traveling alone."

"Thanks."

"No, I mean, I'm really happy. It's fun just being goofy and free. At home I always have to be *so* responsible *all* the time. The kids I teach have *so* many problems—you wouldn't believe how bad it is in high schools now. And I'm always taking care of Elijah and Glen, feeding them, feeding the dogs. Glen's got his falconry, but what have I got? I just clean the house and do stuff for school on the weekends and have dinner ready for *him* whenever he gets home. I keep everything going for everyone else and don't take time to do the things that make *me* happy—like this."

"I think that's why none of the other women came on this trip," I answered.

"Well, now I know why Glen goes off with his hawking buddies almost every weekend—he's following his bliss!"

"And women depend on *men* for *our* happiness."

"Yeah, then we're extremely disappointed because our happiness isn't coming from within ourselves."

"That's what I love about fishing," I said. "Everything about it makes me happy. Planning fishing trips, going to different rivers, standing in them for hours with nature all around you, casting and casting until you're just hyp-notized—God, I *love* standing in rivers. I love fishing with friends. I love fishing alone. I just love fishing. It's bliss. But," I added, "I think it would be double bliss if the man you loved loved to do the things that made you happiest. My idea of heaven would be to fly fish all day and make love all night at all the great fishing lodges in the world. Chile. Argentina. Scotland and Ireland. New Zealand. Costa Rica. Finland. All of Scandinavia. You wouldn't believe the fishing traditions in those places. Dinners are gourmet social events—all silver and crystal and chandeliers. You sleep in antique beds . . . . "

"Built for midgets," Rande said, stirring on her futon, which she had insisted on taking.

"Well, I *love* that kind of elegance after freezing to death in a river all day. It's the *real* me."

"The *real* you needs somebody rich," she laughed.

"The real me needs an intellectual romantic," I replied. "You know: 'Come live with me and be my love / And we will some new pleasures prove / Of golden sands, and crystal brooks / With silken lines, and silver hooks.'"

"Rod McKuen?"

"John Donne! The sixteenth-century English poet."

"I teach art," Rande answered. "All I ever hear is rap music. Someone's gonna kill someone for doing something to his girlfriend, then he's gonna kill his girlfriend. Not very romantic."

"Well, falconry is romantic. Have you ever gone hawking with Glen?"

"Once," Rande replied coolly. "I hated it. When I saw his hawk swoop down and kill that innocent little bunny, it just made me sick. I'll *never* go again."

"But that's *nature*," I protested.

"I don't care. It's not my idea of bliss. And it sure wasn't bliss for the bunny."

"Bliss for the bunny . . . . Sounds like some kind of *Playboy* sex guide."

That got Rande laughing again, but I was worried. How would she feel about jabbing sharp little hooks into the mouths of innocent trout? Fishing, after all, is a blood sport.

~~~~~

The first thing you notice about Steve Smith is that he looks like a handsome Yosemite Sam. The second thing you notice is that he's just as tough. Better-mannered, but tough. He did not put Rande and me in a boat on the river and give us a few fishing tips; he put us into a fly fishing doctoral program, known around western Montana as "Steve Smith's Fly Fishing Torture Chamber." We got handouts, pop quizzes, blackboard sketches—the works. Then *hours* of outdoor casting lessons. Some vacation. If we survived, I knew Rande would do what her students would do: kill me. But at least *I* didn't have to try to teach her how to fly fish.

Smith subjects all his company's fishing school clients to his fly fishing lecture series. And we had to get through it before we could enjoy what we'd come for: one of Smith's famous boat trips down the Middle Fork of Montana's famed Flathead River.

"In fly fishing everything's tapered," he began. "Everything flows from thicker to thinner. This determines the action of the fly rod."

A "fast action" rod, he explained, only flexes from the tip. A "moderate action" rod flexes to the midsection of the rod. "And a 'slow action' rod flexes all the way to the butt."

"That's the Lou Rawls rod," I informed Rande, but she ignored me. Being a teacher herself, she was entranced and already taking copious notes.

Smith, I must say, was easy to watch. He wore a blue work shirt, with black and white heathered suspenders attached to leather buttons sewn onto soiled buckskin-colored canvas pants. His handlebar moustache was as dramatic as the blue glitter in his eyes, and his laugh was deep. His unusual persona helped me retain the parts of his course that were peppered with fly fishing facts and wisdom:

> *Fish like peacock feathers.*
>
> *If you twitch a caddis-fly fly, you get more strikes.*
>
> *Fish hold in front and in back of boulders.*
>
> *Where two currents meet on top, there are fish underneath.*
>
> *The wider the loop, the more inefficient the cast.*

At one point, I leaned over and whispered to Rande: "He forgot something really important."

"What's that?"

"Maxwell's Five Laws of Fishing for Men," I replied.

"OK," Rande sighed. "What are they?"

I wrote them out for her:

> *1. Always set the hook well.*
>
> *2. If he runs, let him. If he's well hooked, he's yours. If not, he was never yours to begin with.*
>
> *3. Never try to reel him in too soon or he'll break your line.*

4. Always maintain some tension or he'll throw the hook.

5. If you get too snagged up, cut bait. There are plenty of fish in the river.

"Hmmm," she said, after reading them over. "You know, Glen ran away after we fell in love. I thought he wasn't coming back."

"But he did."

"Yes."

"Because he was hooked."

"So why did he run away in the first place?"

"Because he was hooked."

"And he came back because he was hooked?"

"Yep. And because he was ready to be reeled in."

"Why was he ready to be reeled in?"

"Because he was tired."

"Tired of what?"

"Tired of fighting the fact that he was hooked."

"And they say *women* are illogical!"

"You must have kept some tension on him, too, right?"

"Well, he wrote me and I wrote him back. Then he called me and we had this long talk and I finally told him I knew we were supposed to be together and it didn't make any sense to be apart and that nobody would love him the way I did."

"And you've lived happily ever after for twelve years."

"Yeah . . . though once it got so snagged up I really did almost cut bait," Rande laughed. "But I haven't met a better trout yet."

Finally, Steve had us practice our knots. Arbor knots for wrapping around the reel spool, "improved" clinch knots for tying flies to the line, and blood knots for building leaders. We were obliged to practice them all while Smith supervised. Rande's blood knot stopped him in his tracks.

"Well," he said after considerable consideration. "It would fish . . . but it would fish weird. You know what the problem is? It's backwards."

~~~~~

Nonetheless, with the *je ne sais quoi* reminiscent of her previous night's pool game, Rande caught the first fish of the trip. It was a beautiful native Westslope cutthroat taken on a parachute Adams fly moments after we put Steve's classic wooden McKenzie River driftboat in at Paola Creek the following morning.

"Pay-ola is right!" Rande sang while she struggled with her reel.

"Tip up!" Steve coached. "Keep the tension on 'im. Let 'im run!"

"Told ya," I told Rande.

Her fish took a nice little downstream screamer and she literally squealed with delight. When it stopped she started cranking with all her get-the-job-done might and just about dredged the poor trout through the water to the side of the boat. It was a wonder that she didn't break him off. But she didn't. When Steve released her wiggly prize unharmed, she gave us a gold medalist's grin.

"That was *fun*," she announced.

"That was *fast*," I replied.

"Well, I wanted to get it over with for the fish's sake . . . but *I* loved it!"

So my compassionate friend wasn't immune to hook-in-mouth disease, but neither could she deny the thrill of the sport of fly fishing. In a Rande-nanosecond she'd figured out a way to have her trout and save it too. We called it "power fishing."

No amount of urging on Captain Steve's part could get Rande to play a fish. She had one style and one style only. She'd whip her rod back and forth in the air like Zorro-in-fast-forward, hurl her line hard into the river, hook a fish, then haul it, wild-eyed and gasping, through the water to the boat. Whip the fly, drag trout, whip the fly, drag trout—that's how Rande fished the rest of the trip. You could hardly call power fishing a blood sport—Rande's fish never bled: all their blood was slammed up against their tails somewhere. Truly, they didn't know what hit them. They didn't have time. And when unhooked they tended to swim away in a dazed, halting fashion.

"Well," Steve said after releasing Rande's fifth trout. "If it didn't have whirling disease before, it does now."

When we pulled over to a little beach for lunch, Steve went off to use the natural facilities and I said to Rande: "Okay, how do you like fly fishing?"

"I like it," she said. "I *love* being out here, and catching fish really is exciting."

"Yeah," I replied. Then, after scanning the area for eaves-droppers, I leaned over and whispered: "You know, I think having a big fish on your line is the closest a woman will ever come to having a hard-on."

Shock registered about a 9.8 on Rande's face, then she began to see the truth of it, and the humor, but mostly the truth. It was true: for a woman, the feeling of holding something as long and powerful as a rod with a fish on the end of it really is almost a sexual experience. And God knows, catching a fish is climactic.

"And they say it's a guy's sport," Rande sniffed.

"Well," I added, "maybe sometimes a fly rod isn't just a fly rod."

The more I thought about it, the more obvious the seduction of fly fishing became. Even the *hope* of catching a fish began to seem erotic. It reminded me of something General Colin Powell wrote in his autobiography, *My American Journey,* about waiting for the bimonthly mail delivery during his first tour of duty in the jungles of Vietnam: "My anticipation," he said, "was almost sexual." There was no smoldering subtext to the statement, no winking implications. It was simply true. Bold, healthy, and true.

Fly fishing *is* sexy. And there you have it.

~~~~~

While we ate our sandwiches, a flotilla of corn-yellow rafts bounced by inches from our boat, filled with happy people in tropical-colored Lycra nymphal cases. Inexplicably, Steve ran over and grabbed an old halibut gaff off the boat's floor, then raised it menacingly in the air. He looked like Captain Hook after a root canal.

"The raft hatch," he arghed. "If they get too close I just say: 'Your boat pops.'"

For the most part, everyone steered clear of "Pop" Smith. Everyone except the fish, which seemed to have a magnetic attraction to our lines. Despite technique problems similar to those she'd had the day before, in Rande's hands a fly rod continued to be as deadly as a pool cue. Together we pulled so many trout out of the Flathead's Middle Fork, it was like rowing in an endless school of flying fish.

We never tired of it, never became blasé. Steve was especially pleased with our obvious glee at each fish we caught.

~~~~~

I never met a fishing guide who couldn't tell a great story, and Steve Smith was no exception. When he sacrificed one of our early trout to the knife so we could ascertain what it was feeding on (caddis larva, rocks and all), Rande and I also learned about a certain long-haired male character who sported wraparound skirts and tank tops and had to be rushed to the emergency room one day because of "a blockage."

"When they cut *him* open, the surgeon fainted," Steve told us. "There was the head of a Barbie doll. In fact, he'd eaten seven of them!"

When the summer heat bade us strip down to T-shirts, Steve recounted the story of an exceedingly large female client who kept stripping off *all* her clothes and diving overboard, but was too heavy to hoist herself back into the boat.

"So I had to haul her in like a giant walrus and she always landed on me. I think she did it on purpose."

The sun kept shining, Steve kept rowing, the fish kept biting, Rande kept power fishing, and I kept refining my hard-won cast. It was different casting from a boat. It felt like being onstage. And that was fine because I knew what I was doing. At least, it felt like I knew what I was doing, and what I was doing seemed to work. Steve would select a fishy spot and anchor up; standing in the bow of his driftboat, I would lean hard into the wooden kneebrace, scan the river for a piece of troutworthy water, and cast to it.

The nice thing about boat fishing is that you almost always have room for an unabridged back-cast, and after months of fighting the Deschutes' riparian thickets this was true emancipation. I had a great time making the longest, tightest loop I could, then launching my line out to some promising seam or pocket water. Accuracy is an easier proposition, too, when casting from a boat, thanks to one's Paul Bunyan stature—you can see better. So I was able to place my fly pretty much where I wanted it, mend my line properly, and achieve drifts even Guido would have been proud of.

Mostly, I fished an Adams that day. It was fun watching the little thing land with minimal plop and float daintily along one of the river's bug lines. Sure enough, hungry trout were waiting there beneath the foam that delineates the union of fast water and slow. More often than not, my fly found its prey, and when it did I'd lift my rod tip the way I'd been taught and, if my timing was good, I'd feel the trout slide gratifyingly into "hooked" position.

Then the fun began. The hard bend made by a fish on the line was, always, a delight in the hand. The weight of it felt forever electric. When the drag sang and a trout took a rocket run just below the water's surface, it made me wonder why they bothered to invent TV. When the fish leaped, my heart leaped with it. Finally, if I hadn't already lost it, I'd try to work it to the boat, responding as best I could to its every move until Steve could get to it and set it free.

The fish we managed to catch that day were small, from

one to two pounds, but each was energetic and tricky, like a powerful little sports car with a very touchy clutch. Some were rainbow trout, wild spawners introduced from California a hundred years ago; some were cutthroats, beautiful natives now being beaten out of their habitat niches all over Montana by rainbows and their exotic brethren, European brown trout and East Coast brook trout, not to mention the toxic fallout from Canadian mining companies. Frankly, the only other fish species I was interested in catching was another native, the bull trout, Montana's answer to Northwest steelhead. The Flathead is famous for them and they can be the size of a prize steelhead—thirty inches, even! It was July, and big bulls would be migrating from Flathead Lake to their many spawning tributaries, but like steelhead, bull trout feed down in the benthic currents, so you have to fish for them with wet flies. And that's not what we were doing. Besides, because of their dwindling numbers, it's illegal to target them anyway. Bull fighting would have to wait.

For now, just having a halfway decent cast was enough of a reward. Even Steve complimented me on my cast. We were all laughing too much to enter the classic Fish Zone, but I didn't care. We were definitely a three-particle system in Steve's wooden boat, and between Montana's nothing-but-blue sky and the scenic beauty beneath it, we bobbed along like a buoyant village nourished by the visual manna of two of the prettiest pieces of wilderness in the West: Glacier National Park to the right, the three-and-a-half-million-acre Bob Marshall Wilderness to the left. The Flathead is an official Wild and Scenic River, and possibilities charge the air with a kind of *eau de sauvage:* at any moment one could see a moose or elk or bear.

"We bugled out a grizzly bear late last year," Steve told us between pulls on the oars. "He looked at us like 'You guys seen any elk?'"

~~~~

On the second day we put in at a place called Cascadilla.

"We're going west fifteen miles to West Glacier," Steve announced. "It's a good long run."

We cruised through the first eight river miles or so, following the same rhythm that had been set up during the early hours of our trip: Steve rowed and I cast at approximately the same speed, which was about half the velocity at which Rande flogged the Rocky Mountain air with her rod. From above I reckon we looked like some old Austrian clock.

Soon the magnificent spire of St. Nicholas rose like the Matterhorn to the east. But down on the river where we were, a fine early mist spread octopuslike over everything, one long pale arm reaching up a creek bed, another exploring an undercut bank.

"I'm gonna tie on Royal Wulffs," Steve said. "You know, white wings in the morning."

"What did you say?" I asked.

"White wings in the morning. The old fly fishing rule: you fish a fly with white wings in low light, so you can see it."

"White wings in the morning," I repeated, enthralled. "That's pure poetry!"

"She was quoting John-John night before last," Rande advised.

"John *Donne*."

"Ah, the English poet," Steve said approvingly.

"See, I *told* you that fly fishermen are romantics. Being surrounded by all this beauty all the time. Birds flying around. That wonderful pine scent. Nature *is* romantic—right, Steve?"

Steve wasn't listening. He was too busy watching the sky. I suspected eagles. Osprey maybe. But all I saw were clouds.

"What's wrong?" Rande asked.

"Well," Steve replied, "The clouds are moving west, but the wind is blowing east. Where I was raised in the Midwest, the biggest storms I ever saw were like that. Whenever you see forces moving against each other, you know you'd better pay attention."

Half a beat later the strangest wind I've ever felt came trumpeting in from the west and spread out over the river like that terrible 1950s footage of the Nevada nuclear test blasts. The water's surface literally crumpled. Steve just kept on rowing. Soon he was rowing with all his might, but we were moving backwards. It had begun to rain.

"Have you ever seen weather this bad?" Rande asked him.

"Once. And not here."

There is no way to get out of the weather in an open boat. Rande and I scrambled into our rain gear and battened down our hoods, but we were both taking on water fast. Gentleman that he is, Steve procured the best protection for us he had: a plastic picnic tablecloth in a gay fruit-salad print.

"I feel like Carmen Miranda on the *Titanic*," Rande said.

"And that's just what you *look* like," I said back.

Sinking in style was a definite possibility: our first big-time white water was fast upon us, a long set of standing waves called Tunnel Rapids, which happened to be the first rapids Meryl Streep ran in *The River Wild*. At the end of Tunnel awaits a surprise, especially for beer-swilling rafters: a wicked vertical boulder called Can Opener.

"Which is much like 'Oh, Shit Rock' on the Deschutes," Steve informed us.

I was glad our boat wasn't made of aluminum.

"Now, if I say 'move right' or 'move left,' *do it,*" he commanded.

Rande and I had failed to mention our mutual directional dyslexia. Now both our minds filled with horrible images of a frenetic Dr. Dick–type scurrying in precisely the wrong direction, followed by a watery death, our bodies marked only by the idiotic shroud of a floating plastic fruit salad.

"I don't swim very well," Rande admitted.

This is because she can do only one thing at a time, arms or legs, not both, so she tends to sink.

"Don't worry, I'll stay with you," I offered heroically.

"Oh, great, a Laurel and Hardy suicide pact. Well, this *is* another fine mess you've gotten us in. *Whoooooooo!*"

We were flying. Despite the handicap of the severe upstream wind, Captain Smith had positioned the boat perfectly. Our rapids debut was rapid indeed. To tell the truth, it was thrilling—because we made it through topside-up and bottomside unopened. We figured we could handle anything after that.

"Next is Bonecrusher," Steve yelled half a mile later.

"Bonecrusher? BONECRUSHER? BONE . . . CRUSH-ER?" Rande and I repeated like a freaked-out witches' chorus.

If you have to be in a boat on a bad rapids during the worst storm in history, it's best if you're with a guide who has earned a lot of nature karma points. Fortunately, Steve Smith's account was in the black. In 1984 he and a nine-strong coalition of wilderness-interest representatives personally stopped one of Montana's most destructive land-use proposals, the deviously named "Wilderness Bill." This black-hearted piece of legislation was sponsored by U.S. Senators John Melcher and Max Baucus, both of Montana. It was designed to decide the disposition of six million acres of de facto wilderness, and baldly opened five million of them to development.

In protest, Smith et al. walked into Melcher's Missoula office and stayed there, occupying all the chairs in the office, forcing the senator and his staff to stand. They just wanted to talk with him, but it took three days to see him, which won them three days of press. Finally Melcher met with them and thanked them for their input. Next the group met with Baucus at his Helena office. He wanted no part of a second office occupation, so he said that while he wouldn't publicly oppose the bill, he would make sure it died in committee. Everyone shook hands on that, the Wilderness Bill did die in committee, and it has been defeated every year ever since.

For their participation in the office occupation, the Montana Wilderness Association gave the group their Art Sedlack Award, an annual tribute to the most outrageous act in defense of wilderness performed in the tradition of Sedlack, the National Park ranger who shot and "killed" an illegal snowmobile in the mid-1970s and made the offending owner pack it out. Smith's group was awarded a chair, "so that Senator Melcher would have a place to sit next time." Clearly, nature owed Smith one. I knew we were safe.

Rande wasn't so sure. When a sideways blast pushed us dangerously close to a boulder, she turned her head inside her rain hood, looked at me whalelike with one eye, and with the resignation of someone recently harpooned, said: "Well, Jess, you never did like to do anything alone. If we gotta go, we might as well go together. Soul-sisters to the end, right? High five!"

We high-fived, but didn't let go of each other's hand, not even when we spotted a photographer atop a house-sized boulder furiously snapping photos of us as we blasted through Bonecrusher. "Hey!" I cried, "we're gonna be in the papers!"

"No, he's our guy," Steve puffed. "He photographs every group that goes by here, even in bad weather. They'll have a proof sheet waiting for you when we get back."

"*Smile,* Rande, *smile!*" I ordered.

The thrill of making it through Tunnel and Bonecrusher settled into a kind of grim resolve as Steve successfully negotiated one stone chute after another. Over and over again we dropped and landed with terrific force while the river hurled ice water at us and the wind slapped us hard in the face.

"Maybe *we'll* be wearing white wings in the morning," I joked, but privately clung to the image of Steve Smith in Senator Melcher's office, mulelike and intractable, not giving an inch, willing a triumphant outcome and bringing it into being.

At one point we passed a yellow raft flipped over and high-centered on a rock. Steve scanned the territory for casualties but there were none; everyone, apparently, had been rescued. For us rescue wasn't an option. If we beached our boat and hiked up to the road, who would get us back to headquarters? We were still miles away from anywhere and there would still be the question of the boat. Should the weather become completely untenable, Steve had promised we'd pull over and wait out the storm, but that could leave us in a perilous state come nightfall. Besides, no craft can handle that kind of abuse better than a McKenzie River driftboat, as the fate of the raft graphically attested. There was nothing to do but sit there and take it.

Steve's first merit badge in Boy Scouts was in rowing. He didn't fail us now. He got us through The Narrows, Screaming Right Hand Turn, Jaws, Pinball, CBT ("Could Be Trouble"), The Notch, and finally Pumphouse . . .

" . . . which is a nice little drop," Steve assured us, "and it's the last one."

The killing tension that had had Steve by the neck all day finally released him, and when it did, Rande and I relaxed too. Our communion was deep, our communication instantaneous. We were through the worst of it and we all knew it at precisely the same moment. Extreme duress must super-correlate particles. "Physical danger that people face and master together bonds them in some mystical way," says Colin Powell. "And conquering one's deepest fears is exhilarating."

I have on my desk a prized photograph of three people in a wooden boat surrounded by leaping white water. One is rowing; two are holding hands and clutching the gunnels for dear life. All are lashed up to their necks in life preservers. The oarsman is hatless, his scowling fatigue obvious even from a distance. The faces of his two passengers are obscured by the brims of baseball caps and hydrocephalic rain hoods. All you can make out are two oddly out-of-place matching grins. And there isn't a fish in sight.

~~~~~

There wasn't a fish in sight at Lee and Guido's wedding a week later, either. But there were clouds. And there was wind. And the two were moving in opposite directions.

The wedding was held on the Rahrs' remote central Montana ranch. Guests were seated on folding chairs in a wild meadow near the edge of a cliff, a good half-mile from the ranch house and its cabins. The Smith River did a slow, green, summer twist far below, and red foxes played in the grasses on the hill to the east.

Lee was beautiful in her white cotton gown, Guido classic in pale linen. He made his vow to her, but before she could make hers to him a slab of demon-sky elbowed its way into the ceremony, growling loudly, spitting venomous rain and hurling lightning pitchforks. At least, that's the way the wedding guests saw it. They gasped and stood in their places, looking up fearfully. Then they began to run. Purses over hairdos, arms around children and the elderly, everyone made the long trot across the meadow and back to shelter. Lee and Guido reluctantly allowed themselves and their wedding party to be shuttled by van to the house. It was as close to living through "Night on Bald Mountain" as I've ever come. Secretly, I loved it. I felt in my bones that this was just nature booming forth its approval.

Back at the ranch, Lee sat in a cabin by a window watching the sky. Outside, Guido waited under the eaves, downing one kirschwasser after another with his brother Willie. Rain water flung itself onto the reception tent in fistfuls. For a while, someone left the cake out in the rain. Disaster seemed imminent.

I found myself standing on a covered porch next to Guido's father, Guido Rahr II, an elegant sportsman who has hunted all over the world. He wore, I noted, a formal German loden hunting coat with antler buttons. I offered my weather theory and he looked startled. He'd been thinking the same thing. "I think it's a show of power," he said. "A vote of confidence. I think it'll clear up soon and things will proceed as planned."

Half an hour later the storm exited stage right and celestial golden light bloomed all around us. Guido and Lee approached their guests and said: "We're ready to get married. And there's only one place we want to get married, and that's out on the cliff. If anyone wants to come, you're welcome."

A loud cheer went up. Almost everyone headed for the cliff, near delirious with relief, post-storm negative ions, and the sheer glory of a day reborn. I snapped an embarrassingly loud Polaroid photo of Lee and Guido finishing their vows. In that heavenly light her dress and his jacket merged, and it appears for all the world as if they're joined at the shoulder by a single pair of blazing white wings.

Chapter Eleven

THE FISH
OF 10,000 CASTS

Summer sprints into fall in the Northwest. Come late July the light goes autumnal. There's a certain slant, a new stillness, a yellowing that wasn't there before. I notice it every year, and every year I think, No, it can't be, it's too soon. But there it is. And there is the reason I began thinking about fishing the Deschutes again only days after Lee and Guido's dramatic summer wedding.

Once fly fishing becomes part of your life, it tends to take over. For me, seasons had begun to affiliate themselves with specific fish and hatches rather than holidays or sports. In winter I think winter steelhead, not Christmas or basketball.

Spring is nymph fishing, the salmonfly hatch, and rainbow trout, not Easter. Summer is Montana, white-winged morning mayflies and August grasshoppers, cutthroats and big browns, not baseball or the Fourth of July. So when autumn rode in on its sifted, unexpected light, my thoughts filled not with pumpkins and turkey or football, but with visions of the October caddis hatch and another chance at a Deschutes steelhead. Secretly I feared it would take a deus ex machina for me to land one.

I was spending more and more time at my mother and stepfather's place on the McKenzie. The pleasure of having a trout stream only steps from your front door is a magnet of inexplicable power. It was like a love affair, really—rivers had hooked me deeply and I couldn't stay away. Now I understood why Carl Jung didn't feel alive unless he lived beside a river. The island in Puget Sound, my protector for so many years, had begun to seem quarantined and apart. But a river was like the heart of something, beating. Perhaps, more accurately, my association with rivers had altered my own internal landscape. I needed connection now, not isolation. I needed an intimate, knowable piece of live water, not a moat.

On the McKenzie I had direct driving access to other excellent Oregon rivers. The North Umpqua is just a couple of hours south of Eugene and east of Roseburg. South of that lay the famed Rogue River, and farther south, on the California border, the superlative Wood and Williamson Rivers that cut through the Serengeti Plain–like beauty of the Klamath Basin. The Metolius River and its difficult Dolly Vardens are just up the McKenzie River Highway a couple of hours from my parents' house. To meet up with Lee and Guido on the Deschutes, all I had to do was keep driving east to Redmond, then head north to Maupin: it was a one-turn trip. Fly fishing had given me a permanent year-round tether to the out-of-doors, but it was the blue lines on the map that gave me a sense of place. I was fast becoming an Oregonian, and there wasn't a damn thing anybody could do about it.

Mostly I just fished the McKenzie, trying to come to know my own home water there. Nights in August and September I'd go just to feel the cool of the river against my legs after the day's heat. It had been hot. Hot enough to open roses until they bent over backwards. Hot enough to dry pantyhose in half an hour, to sweat without moving.

Then one early October morning the iced air of a cold front surprised me, streamers of it moving over my face like magician's fingers reaching through my always-open bedroom windows, pulling me out of the small house my parents let me stay in and down to the river. This new atmosphere and its passel of light rain felt good. It turned the summer-dry cedar deck red, as if it were built out of cinnamon sticks. My mother, who loves cool weather, stopped by for tea. She put her hand in the air and said, "Fall." Then the phone rang. It was Guido. The steelhead were in the Deschutes and he and Lee were heading out. We would meet in Maupin for lunch. I picked up my steelhead rod, General Powell, and headed east.

There was still a thick batting of mist on the river when I left. The water looked like kimono silk, at once smooth and textured; the squat wooden riverfront houses floated in the fog like Buddhist temples. Such a different vista than that of my usual drive south from the island on Interstate 5. I could picture the eastern clouds there at that hour, backlit like splintered glass, then softened by the morning zephyrs until loose wisps blew along the spine of the Cascades like dandelion fur. Then the sun, a perfect gold coin, would lift itself above the clouds like a second sunrise. I could see it shining on the boglands of Centralia, enlightening the political poison of the Midway Butcher's private billboard until its big rectangle glared at passing cars perfectly blank, the color of contemplation, Gandhi's salt, empty, like Bassui's Buddha nature. Or maybe it would read "Love is all there is."

But along the two-lane McKenzie highway there were no billboards. The struggling sun filled the entire east end of the narrow valley and veined its grey marble air with gold. It looked like pictures of old Japan. I so prefer a route whose course mirrors that of a river's over the surgeon's cut of a freeway. Even the chardonnay stink of fresh-pressed road skunk is better than six lanes of exhaust. As the ground vapors broke up they made strange white paisleys against the valley's twin walls of Douglas fir. I do love this river, I thought. I do.

As always, summer had robbed the east side of Oregon of all but the most minimal pigment. The result looked not so much anemic as drained. What was left was husk-color and nutshell, ash white and barn wood and Russell Chatham gold. The Pacific storm cell was moving northeast with me. A few fat raindrops splatted on my windshield like clear-blooded bugs. The desert panorama blurred into a bleached Monet. When a perfect end-to-end rainbow began following my car, its vividness shocked me, like the hot crimson racing stripe on the otherwise pale side of a spawning steelhead. Steelhead, I thought sternly. I've put in my rod hours, paid my dues. It really is time I caught one.

~~~~~

Guido and I fished the Twilight Hole a little that evening. His new wedding band gleamed in the late light. Wearing it, his hands looked more grown-up, more sure. I was proud of him, my chosen brother. Even when he knew he was hooked he hadn't run.

The strong ones never do. When novelist Shawn Wong fell in love with his wife, he didn't run either: "I put the hook in my own mouth," he says, "then I charged the boat." What Guido did was simply to hike Lee up to the ridges right behind us and ask her to make a life with him.

As always, we fished close enough to talk but rarely did.

Eventually I asked him how he liked married life.

"I *love* it," he answered without taking his eyes off his rod tip. "I feel . . . calmer. I feel whole. I feel balanced. It sounds corny, but it's true.

"When you're single and you love rivers as much as I do, you're torn, because if you spend all your time on the water, you never meet any women. You become a fishing monk. All the pretty boys are in town, meeting women at night, then they're around to have lunch with them in cafés the next day. But fishermen blast in and out of town. It's a tough lifestyle if you want to be in the dating loop."

Amazed by this outpouring, I asked my candid coach

what it was like to have Lee on the river with him.

"Oh, I enjoy my life here so much more! Because I can enjoy the woman I love here, too. And I get a lot more sleep. I've gotten more sleep since I've been married than in all the years between college and adulthood combined!"

"Guido, that sounds a little *too* settled."

"No, I just don't go out partying anywhere near as much. Hey," he said, looking up for a moment, "your cast really is better, Max. And that's good, because it's going to get a workout tomorrow. We're going to start early. And we're going to fish every one of my grandfather's steelhead runs. It's going to be a long, long day, and if you don't get a fish I'm going to have to . . . whip you with my 8-weight."

My heart sank like a wet fly. Sweetheart that he is, Guido *is* German, and this sort of thing brings it out—the maniacal focus, the mad-professor tenacity, the fearless absolutism with which he'll go after his goal. Tomorrow was going to be a bear-cat. Fortunately, today was Friday and Guido was tired. We weren't getting any strikes, so we quit the river early and headed back to the house.

About a dozen more people were due in that night, college friends, Portland friends, a set of guys on a Deschutes rafting trip who had dibs on the best lawn camping sites. Guido had gotten permission from his grandfather's widow, Libby Malarkey, to put some of us up in her house next door. It was another wild weekend at Dant, and all I wanted was a steelhead to call my own.

We started at the Twilight Hole again the next morning, mainly because Guido couldn't find one of the fly rods he'd fished there the night before. Sure enough, there was his trusty Winston 8-weight in the brush on the bank. It looked like a magazine ad lying there by the river. I loved its hand-crafted elegance—the rich hunter green color, the walnut-and-sterling silver uplocking reel seat.

"That's *German* silver," Guido pointed out. "That means it's got nickel in it to keep it from tarnishing."

To me the whole thing looked French. A Winston would be at home on the wall above my best antiques. And of course they fish like magic wands. Christmas was coming. Maybe the venerable General Powell would like some new leader-ship for the trout troops?

"OK, now we're going to hike along the Burma Road for an hour," Guido instructed. In wading boots? Yuck. But Guido was giddy about getting me a steelhead. Who else would have taken his pupil's success so seriously? Who else would have stuck with me on this long and twisted journey into casting-hood? Daddy might have, if he'd been a fly fisherman.

If Daddy had been a fly fisherman.

The thought stopped all others. If Daddy had been a fly fisherman, would he have gone to Mongolia with me? Would he have come with us here to Dant? If Daddy had been a fly fisherman and *not* a smoker, I reminded myself, maybe he would have. Okay, if Daddy had been a fly fisherman and not a smoker . . . .

I couldn't complete the image. As soon as I tried, that buried nymphal case of sorrow pushed against my chest again and made my eyes burn. Not now, I said out loud. Not now.

"You don't want to go?" Guido asked.

"Oh. No. Yes. Let's get going."

We hiked to about seven hundred feet above the river, then headed north on the Burma Road, an old sheepherder's path. General Powell pointed the way. Guido had his Winstons, the 8-weight and a lighter trout rod. It was 7 A.M. The sky was still a matte indigo, padded underneath with clouds. Sunrise had laid down an orange strip along the eastern rim of the canyon. The river shimmered below like mercury. We couldn't breathe in enough of that succulent early autumn air, heavy with sage and juniper and the vanilla hay of wild grasses. Every step sent up a fresh draft of it. It was like walking on western potpourri. I couldn't believe this landscape used to make me feel hemmed in.

"Be grateful for the clouds," Guido said. "Otherwise we'd boil in our waders."

Nonetheless, an hour later we were both sweating. My oversized wading boots had given me blisters.

"Okay, there's Slide Riffle," Guido declared finally. "The first good holding water for two miles. Let's go."

The bank was steep and made of loose rock. I followed General Powell's lead but navigated most of the way on my derriere.

"Is this why they call it Slide Riffle?" I asked.

Guido didn't answer. I don't think he heard me. Fishing, as always, compresses his diffuse creative mind into a laser-saber of intention, just like it did my father's. German, Scottish—it doesn't matter. Males of Northern European descent all have Predator's Disease. It's *cold* in that country. You can't exactly walk outside and pick a banana. Back then it was hunt or die. Almost every fly fisherman I know is mostly Celtic or German.

Apparently, Guido's fishing focus also was doing something weird to his lower lip. It had swollen up to unnatural proportions. And he was spitting blood! Really toxic-looking blood.

"Guido, are you OK?" I cried, wheeling him around by the arm.

"Phwhat?" he blubbed.

"My God, are you . . . *still chewing tobacco?*"

It was true. My sophisticated, world-traveling, bookish fishing coach had yet another wad of chew crammed into his lower lip.

"Hi wit schmoking," he gargled.

I was pleased, but this was like fishing beside a poison tree frog. About every third cast a brown sideways geyser would land a few feet from my rod. I took it as a sign to take another step. We fished Slide Riffle a lot faster than usual.

A new wind had arrived out of the west. That Pacific front again. To get my line upstream I had to invent a backhanded cast. "You don't need that much line," Guido advised, in wrangler patois that I had to translate into clear English. "Just start short. Then add line"—spit—"fan out left"—squirt—"covering the water. You want to stay in the strike zone"—pittooee!

My little black Freight Train fly did a respectable imitation of the locomotives that used to run back and forth along the tracks above us, after which this classic Deschutes steelhead wet fly is named. Guido was pleased.

"That swing looks so good, *I* want to jump in and eat it!"

But there were no other takers.

The storm shifted into high. It began to rain. It was cold. My blisters hurt. My hands felt like frozen squid. My mascara ran like squid ink. But this was steelhead weather. We kept moving.

"Put more punch into your cast," Guido called.

"Punch it!" Dr. Dick's voice yelled inside my head.

"This hammer, it rings like silver," Taj Mahal echoed.

"Like *this,*" Guido called.

His lean, green Winston fighting machine hammered the air. Its precious metal butt gleamed in the saturated light. Maxwell's Silver Hammer, I thought. I *had* to get myself a Winston.

But any steelhead rod named General Powell is a powerful weapon, and if power is the cast master in that kind of wind, concentration is the answer to personal discomfort, which is something my rod's namesake learned early in his military career. We were practicing our own version of professional soldiering, as Powell calls it. Or to borrow from the Zen lexicon, a sort of vertical *zazen,* a standing meditation. We had entered The Fish Zone, and an angler in The Fish Zone is a standing wave in moving water. She feels everything. She feels nothing. First there is a blister, then there is no blister, then there is.

By ignoring my body, my mind threw itself fully into its work. The results were masterful. Maybe the fish weren't biting, but each cast I made hit its target with deadly accuracy. This hammer, it rings like silver.

Traditional Chinese doctors guarantee that eventually damp cold will invade warm tissue. When it does, smart mammals seek cover. We hadn't gotten a strike yet and my coach wasn't happy about it. Soon even Guido-the-Sauerkraut could ignore the temperature no more. We had gotten overheated on the hike in, then stood in ice water while our sweat cooled to river temperature and the weather dieties whipped us with frozen ropes. We now occupied the juncture of transcendence and hypothermia. Luckily it happened to be about a hundred yards from Dr. Dick's cabin.

It is telling how comforting even scant shelter is to a life lived out-of-doors. The beat-up wooden shell of Dr. Dick and Roger Bachman's old homestead might as well have been the Ritz. I had blisters as big as the Ritz, anyway, and they were already bleeding. It was nice to get off my feet. I heated water for tea and dug almonds and figs out of my pack while Guido built a fire in the woodstove. Outside the wind howled. By the time I sat down at the table with our two mercifully hot cups, the stove had heated about one square foot of air.

"OK, let's go," Guido demanded.

"We just *got* here!" I wailed.

Therein lies the true difference between female and male anglers: one is graceful, balanced, logical and wise, in touch with nature and all its signals; the other is a rocks-for-brains, infuriating neanderthal.

"I'm *not* leaving until I finish my tea!"

"Then you'll have to visit the bushes all the time."

"No, then I'll be *warm!*"

We compromised. Guido paced while I luxuriously

sipped half my cup. Then we quit the cabin, stopped for a nice, leisurely break de toilette (mine), and moved on down the river. En route to Leaning Tree Hole we passed two guys fishing a nameless little tail water. Their very existence seemed to push Guido over the edge.

"Jet boaters," he said, shaking his head. "Just ignore them."

I averted my eyes to avoid untoward unfriendliness, but jet boats are no friend to a river. The problem is threefold. Their loud, fast presence is antithetical to the aesthetics of Wild and Scenic Rivers, of which, like the Flathead, the Deschutes is one. The noise of jet boats disturbs wildlife; from the rim of the canyon two thousand feet above the river, a passing jet boat sounds like a chain saw not far from your ear. Finally, and worst, research has proven that jet boats seriously impact spawning fish: they spook steelhead, salmon, and trout off their spawning beds, churn up spawning gravel, and damage nests, or redds, thus seriously reducing egg-to-fry survival rates. Fortunately, jet boats have been restricted above Maupin—the fellows we saw shouldn't have been there—but the ecologically enlightened still consider them the scourge of the lower Deschutes.

Leaning Tree Hole was an unproductive exercise. We fished it and the water below it for nearly two hours. At best the fish just weren't hungry. At worst I was missing a lot of serious takes.

With steelhead this is easy to do, and the thought disturbed me. I could not expect steelhead to hit my Freight Train fly like a freight train. Unlike salmon and trout, steelhead strikes generally feel more like a tug on a sleeve. Try it.

Use about as much force as it takes to remove lint. That's what most steelhead strikes feel like. Calling one a "strike" in the first place is like calling chamomile tea espresso: it's just too weak to qualify.

"Why do steelhead make such lame strikes?" I asked my fearless leader.

"It's one of the great mysteries," Guido replied thoughtfully. "They're such an aggressive fish you'd think they'd just slam it," he continued, "but they don't."

"Well, there must be theories." As far as I could tell, fly fishermen had theories on just about everything.

"One theory is that they think the fly is food and they're trying to swallow it. But these are spawning fish," Guido reminded me, "and even though spawning fish don't really eat, steelhead enter the river in July and August and they don't spawn until December or February, even March, so they might eat a little bit to get them through. Sometimes when we cut one open there's some food in its stomach.

"Or it could be they're just playing with the fly," Guido concluded. "Steelhead strikes are just one of those mysteries that are better left unresolved."

It is strange, this steelhead business. Once while our pal Dave Moskowitz was standing on a high bank watching a friend fish the Deschutes below, he witnessed a big steelhead take his friend's fly in its mouth and shake it. His friend never felt a thing.

"That's why the secret is to be in better contact with your fly," Guido explained, "which, of course, men are better at."

I considered hitting him, but any guy raised with three

sisters has mastered being-annoying-as-a-defense, so why en-
courage it?

"The thing to do," he continued, "is to cast more downstream, so your line stays straighter. When you cast across like
we sometimes do, a steelhead could be hitting your fly the
whole time the line's slack, and once the current's straightened it, it could be too late."

It was thoughts like that one that made me want to give
up all hope.

After Leaning Tree we moved down to Malarkey Riffle,
namesake of Guido's grandfather. It's a long piece of fluted
water that looks extremely fishy, but, as I had learned, with
rivers as with guys, looks aren't everything. Personally, nothing we'd fished all day had felt fishy to me. Nonetheless, we
fished Leaning Tree with perfect presence of mind. And I did
my best to keep my line straight without letting my fly drag.
At least the wind had let up.

Over the hours, Guido gave me one new fly after another
to try. Choosing a fly for someone else to fish is a freighted
business. It's akin to, say, telling someone what to wear for a
job interview, or advising them on how to handle a favorite
suitor. Once, while fishing the distant country of Bhutan,
Yvon Chouinard received an unsolicited fly selection from an
unusual source. He was at that moment fishing a river beside
a Buddhist temple, a serious faux pas in this worshipful country. When he looked up he saw a little monk running down
the hill toward him full-speed, robes aflutter. Naturally,
Chouinard thought he was going to be busted. Instead, the
monk grabbed his fly box, rooted around in it for a moment,
then produced a classic Grey Hare's Ear and held it out to

him. Chouinard obligingly tied it onto his line and on the first cast hooked a stellar brown trout, much to the delight of the monk, who stood behind him jumping up and down and clapping his hands.

But there was a distinct similarity among all of the flies Guido had me fish: pale flat wings and orange or yellow somewhere on the bodies.

"They're classic steelhead flies," Guido explained. "Green-Butted Skunks, Hiltons, Freight Trains with their bright pink tag. But you're right, they do look alike. They're all reddish with down-wing patterns, and they have the same silhouette. And it is October caddis time, so maybe we think we're fishing all these special different things, but really all we're doing is fishing caddis-fly pupae!"

A shocking hyena laugh exploded from his mouth along with a startling spray of tobacco. Guido looked like a mad dog. My fishing coach has finally lost it, I thought.

Our final piece of water lay inside the bend of a long riffle. Guido didn't know its name. Underwater boulders there made V's on the surface; they looked like water-arrows pointing back toward Dant. Good idea, I thought. It was almost four. We'd been fishing more than eight hours. Eight hard hours. Eight hard, wet, cold, pretty much miserable hours, except for twenty heavenly minutes in front of Dr. Dick's woodstove, and we had nothing to show for it except more rod hours.

Actually, that's not "nothing." It takes an angler an average of two years to catch his or her first steelhead. It's an amazingly consistent number, two years. Ask anyone. "Yeah, it took me about two years." You hear it again and again.

Usually, when discussing first steelheads, fly fishermen will also say this: "Ah, steelhead. The fish of ten thousand casts." By the end of the day I reckoned I was at least five hundred casts closer.

~~~~~

While I kept sending out reasonably good steelhead casts to an indifferent aquatic universe, Guido fished behind me with the trout rod he'd packed in. This was dangerous. He only had on a four-pound tippet. A steelhead would snap it like a sparrow bone. But given our sorry steelhead record, Guido was nymphing to see if any trout were home, and he was doing it with a Milt Fisher Special—the ol' white yarn strike indicator which, when tied to the line, floats on the surface like a bobber and holds the nymph fly up off the bottom.

Then something odd occurred, as always without warning: a big steelhead attacked Guido's strike indicator! Just rammed it for all it was worth. This also rammed the Steelhead Soft-Take Theory. Guido cast again. Immediately his strike indicator went underwater. He lifted his rod with exquisite finesse, but too much force and the steelhead broke him off. It had indeed taken his fly, but his leader was just too light to handle it.

Breaking a fly off in a fish's mouth is absolutely the worst thing that can happen to Guido on a river. Even though he only fishes barbless hooks, and the hook will decompose in a week or so, while it's stuck in a fish's mouth it can do a lot of damage. To avoid this when steelheading, Guido always builds his leaders out of ten- or twelve-pound line. But this steelhead had gone a-nymphing and ended up with a nasty surprise. I knew it would bother Guido the rest of the weekend. All he said after the incident was, "I feel sick." It was five o'clock. The day was over. Time for our long march home, spent and battered, embarrassingly fishless, and guilty of ruining one fish's week.

Dinner at Dant that night was festive. Libations were generous as always, and good cheer ran through the room like a freight train. Then some retro-dudette put on an old Bee Gees tape from the seventies, and Guido and I found that the natural cadence of casting, mending, and reeling-in perfectly matches the beat of "Stayin' Alive." We dedicated our chore-ography to his steelhead. Line dancing will never be the same.

~~~~~~

Despite feeling barely alive ourselves, Guido and I dragged ourselves back to the Twilight Hole the next morning. Despite my casting director's directions, I did not fish well. I couldn't. I was too done-in by the previous day's marathon. My feet hurt. My casting arm hurt. My casting wrist felt like a freight train was roaring through its carpal tunnel. I hadn't had enough sleep. I hadn't had a shower. I hadn't even had my All One power breakfast. And I was cold. Damn cold. Every cast I made brought me closer to collapse.

I hate this, I thought. Why am I doing this? Why am I standing here in this stupid, freezing river? There are no fish here. No one's caught anything all week! My arm hurts. I'm cold. My face hurts. My *teeth* hurt. Everything hurts. Guido is a slave driver. He won't stop. Only a pea-brain would stand here and do this over and over, day after day, year after year, forever with *nothing* to show for it! That's somebody's definition of insanity. I don't know why I even learned this stupid sport. I DON'T KNOW WHY I SWALLOWED THE DAMN FLY! I probably *will* die!

"Keep casting."

Guido's words fell on my mind like an anvil falling on glass.

My composure shattered. Through hot tears I now saw that he had werewolf teeth and matching eyes and a big black armband on his casting arm, and his fly rod was really a Star Wars laser sword, and that was no Stetson! That was a Darth Vader helmet! In fact, Guido *sounded* like Darth Vader!

"KEEP"—breathe, snort—"CASTING!"

I did, of course. Not only because I was fishing with the Wolfman Fascist Storm Trooper Fish Monster from the Dark Side, but also because I was fishing with my proud steelhead rod, General Powell. If I had quit, not only would Guido have banished me to Planet Remulak but, more important, the General would have been extremely disappointed. As his namesake always says: "If you're going to achieve excellence in big things, you develop the habit in little matters . . . . And always remember that no matter how bad something may seem, it will not be that bad tomorrow."

It wasn't that bad even half an hour later, because to my amazement Guido pronounced the Twilight Hole "dead" and dismissed us from duty. When we arrived back at Dant breakfast was in full—if slow—swing. I dashed over to Libby Malarkey's cabin for a deliciously hot shower, dashed back reborn, and found Lee in the kitchen with the Lucky Charms.

"So how do *you* like being married?" I asked her. (To Mr. Steelhead Gestapo, I added to myself.)

Lee brightened considerably.

"Oh, it's such a blast being married to Guido!" she al-most sang. "It's constantly fun. And you know, I never thought I'd meet someone who loved me as much as I loved him, and to have that romantic energy with someone who's also your best friend—that's a pleasant surprise. But the thing I love most about him is his curiosity. It's so contagious and brings such adventure to our life together. He's such a fasci-nating, energetic person."

He's such a fish-head, I thought.

"Do you think he'd really mind if I left early today?" I said instead. "I'm just fished out. And since he spent all day with me yesterday, I'm sure he'd like some time alone on the water with you."

"Oh, it would be just fine," she said. "And I know how you feel—I can *never* fish as intensely as Guido can. In fact, he already ate and left. He's down fishing right now!"

Perfect, I thought. I packed, said my good-byes, and was back at my parents' place on the McKenzie by dinnertime. I knew I was going AWOL, and I knew I could be court-mar-tialed. But the *real* difference between male and female an-glers is that females know when they need to take a break, and they take it. So I did.

~~~~~

First thing next morning the phone rang. It was Guido and he was not pleased.

"Why did you do that?" he wanted to know. "Why did you leave like that? I was waiting for you down at the river. I can't believe you just took off without telling me."

"I asked Lee," I answered lamely. "She said it was OK." I really was taken aback. Despite his angling obsession, Guido is a kind and mannerly soul. He had never talked to me this way. Ever. He was very, very angry.

"Well, it wasn't OK," he went on. "How do you expect to master this thing if you're not committed to it?"

"I *am* committed to it!" I protested. "I'm *totally* committed to it. I've been studying with you for *two years!* I just needed a break, that's all."

Actually it had been four years since Guido promised to be my fly fishing mentor on the banks of Mongolia's Sharlon River, and I'd really been a serious student for only one year. But I *had* tried to catch a steelhead for two years, and Guido knew it.

"Well, while YOU were taking a BREAK," he hollered, "I went out and caught TWO steelhead. TWO! At least ONE of them should have been yours."

So that was it. He'd invested all this time in me, and when I finally could have earned my stripes I had bailed. I felt terrible. This was our first real fight. I must have said "I'm sorry" about ten times, but Guido just kept hammering me. Nothing I could say now was going to put one of those steelhead on my line where it belonged. If you want to win the big game, you have to suit up and show up. And I had taken the day off. Ugh.

By the time we hung up I felt like a squished salmon egg. I tried to read the newspaper but the words kept swimming away. I did manage to read the fish report: one hundred and seven steelhead had made it over Leaburg Dam. No, I thought, if I go out there and catch my first steelhead here

and without Guido, he really will kill me. I didn't know what
to do with myself.

Then the phone rang again. I made my mother answer it.
It was Lee.

"Lee . . . Rahr?" I asked timidly.

"Lee Lane . . . right now," she replied archly, reverting to
her maiden name. She was not pleased with her husband and
had called to apologize for Guido's call.

"He was way too hard on you," she said. "You didn't de-
serve it and he feels bad that he did it. But he was just . . .
frustrated. You came so *close* to catching your first steelhead.
He just couldn't stand it."

"I *know!*" I sobbed. "I feel *so* awful."

"Oh, well, that's fishing. The thing is, there's only one
Deschutes steelhead trip left this season, and it's pretty close
to Christmas, but I think you'd better go."

As soon as we hung up I called the Winston Rod
Company in Twin Bridges, Montana, and ordered a five-
piece, 7-weight travel rod with a dark walnut-and-German
silver reel seat. I knew she could handle a big Deschutes steelhead just fine. And I knew what I was going to name her:
Winnie. "Win," for short.

~~~~~~

The plan was to drive to Portland, pick up Guido and Dave
Moskowitz, and head over Mount Hood to Dant. We were
three-quarters into December, it was midweek, and the temperature on the McKenzie was in the thirties; the east side of
the mountains would be colder. We reckoned we wouldn't
have much competition on the Deschutes.

I was staying at my parents' place for the holidays. My California sisters were already there with their husbands and my nephew and niece. Getting out of tightly woven Christmas plans was tricky. No one else in my family fishes, so the priority status of this particular steelhead trip was hard to explain. "Just think of it as my bar exam," I told Heather, my attorney-sister, meaning that there was a bar just past Freida's Riffle I wanted to examine.

"If I don't go, my fishing coach will become autistic," I told Valerie, my psychologist-sister, meaning that Guido would never speak to me again.

~~~~~

"So, you wanna hear the latest report from the river?" Dave Moskowitz asked once we had all piled into Guido's old VW van. "Three fish. Two on, lost both, the other one just a pull."

Actually hooking a steelhead is so rare that steelhead anglers count fish-to-the-fly.

Guido was in a terrific mood. He had already apologized several times for what we still refer to as his "Rush Limbaugh Phone Call." I told him I considered it a natural release, a show of power and a vote of confidence, like the wedding storm. Privately I had vowed never to get him that riled again.

It was doubly pleasing that Dave had come along. Every time he'd been on a fishing trip I'd caught a fish. He was *my* Lucky Charm.

While I hadn't said anything, I was taking this trip very seriously indeed. I had, in fact, declared war on my standing steelhead record, and on my low steelhead expectations. I was going into this battle to win, just like General Powell says you should: "Go in with a clear purpose, prepared to win—or don't go." Therein lay the fundamental error of my earlier steelhead battles: I hadn't cared enough about winning. I had cared too much about casting, not enough about catching fish. It was an attitude I needed to correct. To that end, I had in my old metal rod case my new secret weapon: Winnie, my gleaming as yet unfished Winston 7-weight.

It was good being at Dant when it was so uninhabited. Good but strange. I was used to that old tribal sense of people coming and going, of lights on in the other houses, of running into Dr. Dick on the river and wishing the occasional unknown angler who showed up would just go away. There was a bittersweet peace to it all now. I liked it.

Guido, Dave, and I went about our settling-in in a serene fashion. There was no pressure to organize dinner for hordes, you didn't have to hawk-eye the bathroom for vacancies, and everyone got their own bedroom. It was nice. And it matched the mood of the land. Winter had thrown a frosty glamour over everything. Things had slowed way down. A contracted sensibility reigned supreme, as if a triangular block of anesthetic gas now plugged the deep V of the canyon. There was no wind. Nothing moved. Without leaves the skeletal remains of the cottonwoods and alders stood at river's edge frozen in heavenly salute. One thing was sure: it was going to be some frigid fishing.

We all were up early the next morning. Outside the light looked lavender with chill, as if one were viewing the world through a thin veneer of ice. "Hoh boy," I thought, and dug out my wool hat and scarf. I still didn't own the right angling ensemble, but who cares what you look like while reeling in a big steelhead.

Guido and Dave were outside at the picnic table gearing up. With great inner exuberance but no external fanfare, I opened my old metal rod case and drew forth my new rod from its cloth sheath.

"Whoa," Guido breathed. "Where'd you get that?"

Winnie's finely crafted ferrules slid together with a gratifying click. Once assembled she glowed in that wintry air like forged steel. I didn't know where my delight in her deadly beauty came from. Surely somewhere deep in my Scottish soul, some half-remembered song of the warrior passed from the early Maxwell males even to this modern clanswoman. My pride runneth over.

Guido wanted to fish Twilight Hole first. By now it was a tradition. Why not? The Twilight ranks as one of the most productive steelhead holds on that piece of the upper Deschutes, and its easy proximity to the house didn't hurt.

"That's an upstream cast," he reminded. "You want to cast straight across, mend the line, and let it swing down slowly."

My next cast was terrible. I was all nerves. I felt like an Olympic athlete who had prepared years for this moment. Everything rode on it. Ecstasy and devastation hovered like adversarial spirits, making me dizzy.

Guido was his princely patient self again, maybe more so than usual. This time *my* state of mind was the problem.

Guido had given me the upstream position. While he worked with his new casting giant, a ten-foot Scottish spey rod that required two hands to cast, I flailed with Win. She behaved like the professional that she is, smooth, fast, and responsive, despite my errors. She and I fished a classic Deschutes black steelhead fly called a Coal Car; Guido and his spey rod fished an orange-bodied General Practitioner.

Dave was spotting for us from the railroad tracks above. Suddenly he yelled. A big steelhead was bird-dogging Guido's fly. Then it took it. Dave yelled again. The fish threw the hook and vanished as if the strike had never happened.

Now my nerves had nerves. "This is it, you dope," I told myself. I was right: there were fish in the river, there was no competition, and it was my last chance. It was now or never.

I cast. Another lousy cast. Then I got snagged up. I remembered Guido's easy desnagging technique of just letting out more line until the current pulls your hook free for you from the opposite direction, which it usually does. It did. I cast again. And got snagged up once more. There is a lot of woody debris in the lower Twilight Hole. This makes for quality habitat, but it's hell on hooks.

I finally worked that cast free, then Guido commanded me to reel in. I thought I was being court-martialed, but he only wanted to change my fly to a classic General Practitioner. My Scottish proclivities liked the idea, but given my current dementia nervosa I knew it wouldn't make much difference.

"Just fish it like you know how," Guido said, patting me on the shoulder.

Fish it like I know how. As in "as if you know how" or "the way you know how." Could I fish or couldn't I? Did Guido think so or didn't he? First there is an angler, then there is no angler, then there is. I was so twitterpated, I couldn't remember how to pull my fly off the water to make another cast.

While I stood there practically drooling with paralysis, a beautiful emerald-headed mallard came in for a skating landing on the opposite side of the river. What he was doing there that late in the season, I'll never know. But I do know he was a messenger from the fish gods, because he reminded me of perhaps the most important lesson-by-example I've ever learned. And it had to do with skating and the Winter Olympics.

Katarina Witt and Deborah Thomas were in a dogfight for the gold medal. Canada's sprightly Elizabeth Manley was a shoo-in for the bronze. Katarina made her decisive performance and was brilliant; her win was cinched. Deborah entered the rink and caught a blade on the ice. It was all downhill for her after that. It hurt to watch.

Then it was Elizabeth's turn. She arrived on the ice smiling, and proceeded to skate like an angel. The crowd was stunned, the applause deafening. Had she skated like that from the beginning, she would have taken the gold herself.

As it was she took the silver. When she was interviewed on camera afterward, she was asked what happened. "Well," she replied, "I was getting all caught up in the competition between Katarina and Debbie, so I went to a counselor. And she said, 'Just skate for the reason you started skating in the first place. Skate for the joy of it.'" So she did.

I turned and looked at Guido. Just as in Mongolia, I saw his elegant line write my name again on that western sky, but this time there was a second part: "You love this sport. Fish like you love it."

Of course. Fish for the joy of it! For the love of it. Fish for all the bottom-line reasons anglers do what they do. The rest will take care of itself.

I breathed in, pulled myself up out of my own muddle, and practically strangled Win in my grasp. I cast. And got snagged up. Then that big, heavy hunk of underwater rotten log leaped out of the river like a piece of rising moon. A steelhead. An honest-to-God, live-to-tell-the-story, shimmering Deschutes steelhead. Win had a win on her hands.

And I had trouble. This fish was serious. Serious about having a hook in its mouth and serious about not liking it. After its aerial display, the old mariner turned and went speeding toward Washington State.

My early salmon training kicked in. This fish is *not* getting away from me, I thought. I know how to play a fish. I knew to let it run. I knew to try to turn its head. I knew to keep my fingers away from my screaming, knuckle-busting reel handles. But the anticipation of a suddenly limp line made me sick to my stomach.

The line on my reel was doing a Houdini disappearing act. The steelhead was almost pulling Win's strong brown reel seat clean out of my hands. I had no choice but to chase my fish.

Then I was flying, too, hurdling boulders, skipping branches, clunk-zipping along in my impossible boots, splashing like a silly seal, feeling more as though the fish were playing me.

Then I *was* being taken, taken not by the fish but by my father's hand, his strong brown hand. I remembered! Flying behind him while he raced down the beach, sprinter that he was, the surf engulfing his ankles. Valerie's right hand in his left, my left hand in his right, our little-girl feet practically walking on water. He was, in those fleeting moments, our engine, the one who took us, who moved us, who guided us as we flew there beside him, flew *because* of him. In those speeding seconds, the power of our connection to our father was completely with us, we were completely his, and he, for once, was ours.

In the wake of that forceful memory the nymphal case of sorrow rocked and broke. Grief flew out of my mouth on silent stuttering wings. Dad. Dee. Dad-dee. Daddy. Tears and river water met upon my face, salt and fresh, the twin homes of all anadromous fish. I had left my own on one to find my own on the other, the far edge of the Pacific pushing me inward always toward the heart, toward intimacy, toward the close power of the Deschutes and now the McKenzie. Two rivers and an ocean. My own watery triangle circumnavigating my private triad: the father and the daughters, Daddy, Valerie, and me.

Guido says I played the steelhead with unexpected grace, but I remember it not. My mind was gone to the joy of the memory of what was for a moment so long ago but couldn't last, and to the pain of what could have been but wasn't. I missed beyond words the father I never had. There is true heartbreak for all of us who loved fathers who could not love us back, but then there is the necessity of looking as well at what has been given instead in order to avoid the crippling fallout of self-pity. My father had given me the natural world, an abject love of it and an absolute need of its enchantment. He had given me the template of adventure, the matrix of the grand fishing trip. Really, he had given me this fish. This fish pulled that out of me as I flew downstream with it, flew until we both tired, until it turned finally and I could reel it home.

There are photos to prove it, Guido grinning, holding the steelhead, a stunning eight-pound buck with a pink comet blasting down each flank, me smiling a shell-shocked smile, my new rod, Win, proudly at my knee. Held horizontally low in the frame, the steelhead forms the base of the new triangle: fishing coach, fisherwoman, and fish. Guido says when he reached down to remove the hook it just fell out of the steelhead's mouth. He says that means the fish chose me. But I only knew what the fish taught me: that on this slippery physical plane, where hearts beat steadily or they don't, we had better fish hard and fish to win, fish right up to Bassui's moment of enlightenment when we become like a log thrown into a fire, our whole body ablaze without being aware of heat, as long as we remember, always, to fish first for the joy of it.